How to Be a
Hollywood Star

ALSO BY STEPHEN P. WILLIAMS

How to Be President

How to Be a Hollywood Star

Your Guide to Living the Fabulous Life

♦♦♦

STEPHEN P. WILLIAMS

THREE RIVERS PRESS • NEW YORK

Three Rivers Press and the Tugboat design are registered trademarks of Random
House, Inc.

Library of Congress Cataloging-in-Publication Data
Williams, Stephen, 1958–
How to be a Hollywood star: your guide to living the fabulous life /
Stephen P. Williams—1st ed.
1. Motion pictures—Humor.   2. Motion picture actors and actresses—Humor.
I. Title.
PN6231.M7W55 2006
791.4302'07—dc22

ISBN-13: 978-0-307-33622-4
ISBN-10: 0-307-33622-0

Printed in the United States of America

Design by Nora Rosansky
Illustrations by Nancy Leonard

10 9 8 7 6 5 4 3 2 1

First Edition

For my young stars—

Bolivia, Emelia, Violet,

and Beckett

Contents

Introduction 15

Acronyms and Definitions 17

CHAPTER 1

Welcome to Hollywood: A La La Land Primer...... 21

The Great Divide...... 21

Star Knowledge: Where to Live...... 23

Star Issue: How to Select a Home 25

What Is This Feng Shui Stuff? 26

Duties of Household Help...... 27

Vetting Your Nanny...... 28

Helpful Household Phrases for Spanish-Speaking Employees...... 28

Sexual Harassment 29

Star Question: Is It True What They Say About Pool Technicians? 31

Star Issue: PSYOPS, or Nonlethal Methods for Coping
with Driveway Tourists 31

Six Signs of a Stalker 32

The Stalker Personality 32

License to Carry 33

Star Question: How Do I Coordinate My Gun with My Wardrobe? 34

Defensive Clothing 35

The Entourage or Posse 36

Hollywood Secret: Endow Now...... 36

Preemptive Birthing 37

Star Birth Center 37

Playtime 38

Star Pets and Their Meanings 38

Lost Animals...... 39

Getting Around 40
Armored Vehicle 40
Star Knowledge: In the Drive 40
How to Hire a Driver 41
Hollywood Secret: Service Station to the Stars 42
Earthquake Risk 42
Star Question: Where Can I Buy a Richter Scale? 43

CHAPTER 2

Social Life: How to Stay Centered When Everyone Envies You 44

Peers, Pests, and Other Personalities 44
Entertaining at Home 45
The Price of Gossip 45
Guest Formula for a Great Dinner Party 47
Great Dinner Party Guest Density 47
Ideal DP IG Seating Chart 48
Dinner Table Conversation 49
Star Knowledge: The All-Purpose Menu 49
Proclivities and Propensities 50
Swag 50
Dog Run Socializing 51
Canine Coitus 51
Star Issue: Dating a Nobody 52
Satisfying Short-Term Sexual Urges 53
Hollywood Secret: Hooking Up with Fellow Stars or Industry Players 53
Engagement: Traditional Values Predominate 53
Buying Rings 54
Star Knowledge: How to Suggest a Prenup 55
The Wedding 56
Self-Esteem Index 57
Wedding Mechanics 58
Star Issue: Homemade Sex Tapes 58

The Sex Set 59

Star Question: Who Is My Friend? 59

Supportive Friends or Friends You Support? 60

CHAPTER 3

Self: Improving Your Mind and Body Goes with the Job 61

Controlling Your Reflection 61

Star Power 62

Daily Diva Affirmations 62

Ten Common Physical Flaws 65

Star Knowledge: Turn Your Ass into an Asset 66

**Plastic Surgery Options Examined for Cost, Procedure,
and Recovery:** A Look at Some Common Surgeries 66

Determining if You Are Compatible with Your Plastic Surgeon 70

BDD 71

Common Personality Flaws 71

Star Issue: Hiring a Life Coach 73

Star Question: Are You Driven by ADHD? 74

Cigarettes, Heroin, or Coffee? 75

Legal High 76

Star Question: What Should I Pack for Rehab? 77

Rehab Amenities 77

Star Issue: Celebrities Anonymous 78

Star Knowledge: Upbeat Answers to Press Questions
Regarding Your Rehab 78

Inner-Child Care 79

Celebrity Worship 79

Hollywood Secret: Using Religion to Your Advantage 81

CHAPTER 4

Milking It: Self-Exploitation for Fun and Profit 83

Honoring Your Inner Publicist 83

Self-Exploitation 84

Hollywood Secret: Walk of Fame Demystified 85

Star Knowledge: The Publicist.. 85

The Truth... 86

How Gossip Gets into Circulation... 87

Developing a Silver Tongue.. 88

Monikers.. 89

How to Tell a Joke... 90

Anatomy of a Talk Show 91

"This Is an Outrage!": Pros and Cons of Expressing Anger 92

Star Issue: To Be or Not to Be (Gay) 92

Marriage of Convenience 94

Ten Surefire Attention-Getters 94

Dos and Don'ts: Arrest.. 95

Star Knowledge: Hiring a Prison Coach 95

Food for Thought 96

Political Exploitation 97

Star Question: May I Have an Ideology? 97

Setting Parameters (and Perimeters) 98

Good News About Journalistic "Integrity" 98

Star Knowledge: How to Air Kiss... 100

Star Issue: Handling the Paparazzi 101

A Paparazzo Speaks... 102

Hollywood Secret: Racketeering 103

Ten Reporters' Questions You Should Always Answer with a No........... 103

From Idea to Printed Page 104

When to Lie Low.. 105

CHAPTER 5

The Grind: Six Days a Week, Six Weeks in a Row, for Only $16 Million........................106

Work Is What You Live For 106

How to Behave 107

Movie Production Timeline... 107

On-Set Hierarchy... 108

How to Act 108

Character Acting 109

Star Issue: Danger 109

Stunts 109

Downtime 111

Personal Assistants 111

Ten Tasks Fellow Stars Have Delegated
to Their Personal Assistants 112

Star Knowledge: Anatomy of a Screenplay 112

Technical Aspects of the Script 113

The Popcorn Factor 113

Film Festivals 114

Negotiating the Cannes Film Festival 115

Star Question: What Should I Pack for Cannes? 117

Star Power: Exploiting Your Own Charisma 117

Romania: The New Burbank 118

The Studio Jet 118

Star Knowledge: The Kiss 119

Star Issue: Exposure 120

Credits 121

Star Perks 121

Hollywood Secret: The Star Wagon Supreme 123

CHAPTER 6

Money: Getting What You Deserve 124

Money Is the Hollywood Art 124

Studio Revenues 125

Blurry Image 125

What an Agent Does 126

Star Issue: How to Fire an Agent 127

Average Star Salaries 127

Anatomy of a Movie Deal 128

Sample Earnings 129
How to Justify Your Existence 129
Star Knowledge: Stop Dates 130
Blockbuster 130
The Budget 130
Studio Accounting Practices 131
Selling Out, Discreetly 132
Star, Inc. 133
Product Branding 133
The Two Basic Hollywood Paths 134
Star Issue: Fees 134
Hollywood Secret: The Happy Mailbox 134
Annual Star Expenses 135
Star Knowledge: Nonfinancial Remuneration 136
Hollywood Stock Exchange 137
Star Issue: Switching from Movies to Television 137
Hollywood Secret: The Black Card 137
The Golden Statue 138
What Is an Oscar? 139
Oscar Swag 139

CHAPTER 7
Leisure: Successful Relaxation Requires a Lot of Work 141
Even Stars Need a Break 141
Star Knowledge: Bowling 142
Hollywood Secret: Shop Naked 143
Star Issue: Buyer Beware 143
Star Superfans 145
Foreign Escapes 146
Flying Commercial 146
Star-Class Seating 147
Star Knowledge: The World's Most Expensive Lunch 148

Pros and Cons: Private Vacations vs. Media Circus Vacations 149

Vacation Locales 149

Dos and Don'ts: Leisure Wardrobe 150

Collecting Art 150

Star Issue: Kidnapping 152

Star Risks 153

Yachts 153

The Star Yacht 155

Paparazzi Control at Sea 155

CHAPTER 8

Taking a Bow: Life and Death Issues 156

Illuminate Your Fading Star 156

Star Issue: Life Span 156

The Wisdom of *Sunset Boulevard* 158

Hollywood Secret: A Living Legacy 159

Star Issue: Failure 159

Star Cemetery 160

Star Departure 160

Star Knowledge: Death Notices 161

Ten Appropriate Star Epitaphs 162

Hollywood Star Quiz 164

Acknowledgments 173

Introduction

CONGRATULATIONS. YOU'RE GOING TO BE A STAR.

Your major studio release opens Friday. Soon you'll be flying in private jets, using your four-band cell phone to conference from *Lago di Como* with your accountants, and receiving designer gowns via courier. Welcome to the club.

This manual is the first, and most important, perk you'll ever receive. Legend holds that this little-known document has been presented to all new Hollywood stars since first being compiled in 1927 by associates of Louise Brooks after *Rolled Stockings* shot her into the limelight. The luminaries of each succeeding generation have updated the manual with comments and corrections. Please keep the information confidential. Have your personal assistant (PA) make notes in the margins: As your star power (SP) dims, you, too, will be asked to update this manual for the generations of stars waiting to take your place. Enjoy the ride! (Always sit in the backseat.)

Acronyms and Definitions

ACJ aggressive celebrity journalist

ADHD attention deficit hyperactivity disorder (fame-induced)

awareness mission public relations campaign

barnacles entourage members

BDD body dysmorphic disorder

beighborhood neighborhood with lots of good-looking people

BR board (surf, skate, snow) rider

CGS closeted gay star

CS compulsive shopping

CU celebrity urinalist (negative colloquialism)

DIZO dual income zero orgasm

DPGD dinner party guest density

ER entertainment reporter

FNP failed negative person

FSF foreign superfan

FSM financial services mogul

GDP great dinner party

GDPGD great dinner party guest density

GP gift porn

helicopter mate who hovers, always

IARAM innocent, ambitious, recent arrival from the Midwest

ID intellectual director

IG invited guest

ILE Ivy League egghead

IP industry player

LAPD Los Angeles Police Department

lavender marriage marriage between a CGS and an opportunistic partner or fellow CGS to avoid homophobic publicity

LI lesser invitee

LMS last-minute shortage

luxyon canyon full of luxury homes

MCB mixed creative bohemians

MFPS male or female porn star

nontourage cluster of nobodies at celebrity hotspot

NS no-show

NSSI no-show star invitee

OPF obsessed predatory fan

PA personal assistant

PH player hater

PHAF pretty and heavily accented foreigner

PPC personal production company

RAPAP rabid paparazzi

RGMA reformed gang member or addict

rock basketball

ROW rest of world

RP regular people

SA sharklike agent

SF superfan

showflake person who is chronically late

SI star invitee

SLAL star look-alike

S&M studio money

sodewha socialite, designer, whatever

SP star power

SS star shill

teenile person who is too old for their clothes

TG top gossiper

TP team player

Trustafarian dreadlocked trust-fund child

WAR wire access roaming

How to Be a
Hollywood Star

CHAPTER 1

WELCOME TO HOLLYWOOD

A LA LA LAND PRIMER

THE GREAT DIVIDE

There are two places called Hollywood.

1. Physical Hollywood hugs the Santa Monica mountain range in Los Angeles and is accessible by compact car from Laurel Canyon Boulevard, the 101 Freeway, and Santa Monica Boulevard. A brief history: In 1886, a crippled Topeka, Kansas, man named Harvey Wilcox bought 160 wilderness acres outside Los Angeles. His wife, Daeida, christened the ranch "Hollywood," after an Ohio town someone had mentioned on a train. In the early 1900s, movie companies were drawn to Hollywood's intense sunlight. They also liked its distance from the New Jersey courts where inventor Thomas Edison had filed lawsuits claiming copyright ownership of the filmmaking process. Edison lost and the studios prospered.

   The first Academy Awards took place in 1929. In 1960, the first star was laid in the Walk of Fame. Currently, about three hundred thousand people live in Hollywood, including many homeless teenage

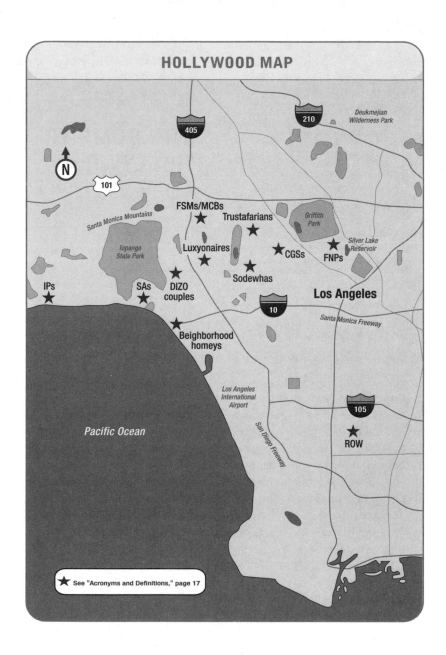

HOLLYWOOD MAP

N

101

405

210

Deukmejian
Wilderness Park

Santa Monica Mountains

FSMs/MCBs
★

Trustafarians
★

Griffith
Park

Silver Lake
Reservoir

Topanga
State Park

Luxyonaires
★

★ CGSs

FNPs
★

★
Sodewhas

IPs
★

SAs
★

DIZO
couples
★

Los Angeles

10

Santa Monica Freeway

★
Beighborhood
homeys

Los Angeles
International
Airport

Pacific Ocean

San Diego Freeway

105

★
ROW

★ See "Acronyms and Definitions," page 17

hustlers, a few long-legged farm girls, and several Armenian shop owners. Most of the studios are now in Burbank and elsewhere. As a star, you might pass through this community on occasion for business or entertainment purposes, but it will not be your home.

2. Magical Hollywood, which you will inhabit, crosses geographical boundaries to include parts of Los Angeles, New York, France, and Montana; the first-class lounges of international airports; nightclub VIP rooms; hyperyachts; and secluded, pampering resorts in odd locations. You may reach this Hollywood only via jet, helicopter, comfortable boat, motorcycle, or late-model Maybach. In this Hollywood, people eat raw foods, wear thousand-dollar T-shirts, and bemoan their loss of creative freedom. It is a world that only you and your peers will ever understand. Once inside, you will do anything to stay.

STAR KNOWLEDGE: Where to Live

Star abodes fall along a line stretching from Silver Lake, at the intersection of the 101 and 5 freeways, west to Santa Monica and up the coast to Malibu. A number of desirable communities lie within this geography, and each has its own personality and implications for your image.

Los Feliz/Silver Lake: This area is suitable for stars who haven't left their roommate days behind. If you're still here when stardom calls, move immediately to negate the risk of running into failed negative people (FNP) who haven't made it big. You deserve better, unless you're purchasing one of the pedigreed midcentury modern homes bordering the reservoir. If the realtor drops the names Richard Neutra, Rudolf M. Schindler, Gregory Ain, or John Lautner, immediately offer the full price, as houses by these dead architects confer great status.

West Hollywood: More a shopping and dining destination for stars than a place to pitch a tent. This is Gay Hollywood. If you are a closeted gay star (CGS) in this neighborhood, be prepared for paparazzi and make sure your lifestyle denial speech is well-scripted.

Mulholland Drive: This legendary winding road is lined with glamorous homes perched high above the city. Away from the madding crowd and far from good takeout restaurants, this area is perfect for stars who are comfortable in their skin and who like the freedom to tinkle in their backyards, if the urge hits them, without upsetting the neighbors.

Laurel Canyon: The side streets of this canyon have been home to superstars, porn stars, politicians, and drug dealers. The jumbled compounds are perfect for bohemian sensibilities and substance-addled Trustafarian souls. Neighbors will applaud your spiritual commitment when you install a large stone Buddha that dribbles water out of its mouth into your pool.

Beverly Hills: While the neighborhood certainly has cachet, it's also less inviting and more crowded than a true star might appreciate. These days, Jed, Jethro, Granny, and Elly May would more likely be known as the Bel Airbillies.

Bel Air: Now you're talking. The astounding amounts of water consumed by the picket-fence roses in these arid luxyons mark Bel Air as true star territory.

Brentwood: This double-income-zero-orgasm (DIZO) neighborhood features big houses, big egos, and strong gates. You might bump into your agent here. The sidewalks are so deserted that stars have been known to murder their cheating spouses right on the street and get away with it.

Pacific Palisades: Urban legend holds that families who live in this wealthy neighborhood of fresh air and tranquil homes stay together longer than families who live in Beverly Hills.

Santa Monica: A beighborhood home to surfers, flower children, and power-hungry vegetarians, this casually expensive beachside community is perfect for socially aware stars.

Malibu: Seemingly simple cottages on stilts line the beach, but be assured that luxury reigns behind their charming facades. High-wattage stars work hard to keep riffraff off the beach so they can play fetch with their dogs in peace. Check deeds for public beach access stairways before purchasing a home here, or you might end up having to file a lawsuit to remove the permanent gathering of fans just below your deck.

STAR ISSUE: How to Select a Home

Your career success depends, in part, on your home. An unseemly home (too small, too ugly, too far from power-lunch spots like the Ivy) will mark you as antisocial and unpredictable, which are undesirable traits in an industry of team players. Aim for a beautiful house that's as unapologetically large as your ego. Choose from among the following styles:

Tudor: These houses, which feature cosmetic, nonstructural wooden beams, steeply pitched roofs, and stucco walls, became popular in the 1920s when Lon Chaney, Louise Brooks, and Charlie Chaplin reigned supreme. To Americans, the style has always evoked visions of English country homes. To everyone else in the world, fake Tudor just looks dark and dumb. Leave these houses for the Film Theory 101 professors. Tudor does not have star power (SP).

Tiki: This Hawaiian lounge look is good for young Hollywood stars. You can trade up to something more mature after your twenty-third birthday.

Mayan Revival: Serious architects are still in awe of this exotic motif from the 1920s that radiates creative power. Best for eccentric stars.

Midcentury Modern: Perfect for your weekend getaway home in Palm Springs. Reflecting pools, metal arches, airport-lounge-style sloped ceilings, overtiled bathrooms, curved colorful chandeliers, and stone walls tell the world you have arrived and are proud to be cool. Expect major magazine attention. Star friends may be a bit bored, as this trend is peaking.

Postmodern: No one knows exactly what this term means, except that it is the condition of postmodernity, or "after what is now." But enough theory. In practice, postmodern houses make unashamedly bold and goofy statements, with oversize columns, vaguely historical windows, shingle siding, and perverted traditional forms. Favored for East Coast star retreats like Easthampton and Martha's Vineyard. Perfect for auteurs.

Spanish Revival and Mission: These stucco houses with red-tiled roofs are always right for any Hollywood star, and they look good in *Architectural Digest*.

Bungalow: Low-key Los Angeles architectural form that works well for young star couples on their way up.

Minimalist: For secure stars only. This highly evolved style eschews ornamentation and color, relying instead on clean open spaces that say, "I am so successful that I need nothing." While the houses invariably look empty, there are always many hidden closets and drawers for concealing star junk.

WHAT IS THIS FENG SHUI STUFF?

This ancient Chinese philosophy is an unlikely source of glam design in LA, but it has influenced everything from the Getty Center art museum to Laurel Canyon meditation rooms. Feng shui (pronounced "fung shway") is based on a Taoist understanding of how the forces of nature work together to create harmonious environments inside the home. In Chinese, *feng* means *wind* and *shui* means *water*. Good feng shui leads to good fortune, and bad feng shui—you don't want to go there. You may hire a feng-shui master (see the Los Angeles yellow pages) to study the flow of energy through your new home and help redesign the interior or even make structural changes to improve your (already great!) fortune.

According to Eva Wong, a Hong Kong–born feng-shui expert, here's how to hire a feng-shui person:

Decide whether you want a traditional practitioner or a New Age feng-shui practitioner. The traditional experts follow centuries-old beliefs, whereas the New Age experts have only recently adapted the science to

Western culture's need for harmonious placement of dog beds, tread-mills, and Oscar statuettes.

Choose either a Chinese practitioner or someone who is very familiar with Chinese culture.

Choose someone who will explain the rationale behind every recommendation. If you are going to install a five-ton boulder near the front door, you'll want to know why.

DUTIES OF HOUSEHOLD HELP

Good help isn't found, it's made. With the proper resources—money, manipulation, and power—you can turn even a mediocre domestic staff into a living, breathing reflection of your own grandeur. Begin by communicating to your employees the exact nature of their duties and responsibilities. Nothing is more frustrating, or more wasteful of your valuable time, than dealing with unmet expectations. Here are the duties of the major household staff positions you will need to fill.

JOB	DUTIES
Majordomo or butler	*Make sure everything works; dress in black to impress guests; keep guests from poaching staff.*
Lawn and garden person	*Keep things green; mix in other colors as needed; report paparazzi in bushes.*
Pool person	*Have a trim and muscular physique; maintain hygiene of hot tub; never stare at poolside nudity; fulfill miscellaneous intimate functions depending on employer's unmet needs/desires.*
Maid	*Always look down while cleaning; pretend to be charmed when guests* habla *with mangled syntax.*
Chef	*Read latest diet books; lie about calorie/fat/carb content of meals served.*
Property manager	*Keep property immaculate; never notice unusual behaviors; take the Fifth when necessary.*

Nanny	*Feed, clothe, bathe, cuddle, and put to bed the children; cede bragging rights to parents.*
Driver	*Sit in car until needed; keep eyes on road, not on backseat; assume role of therapist during traffic jams.*
Security	*Look strong; look the other way; share protein powder as needed.*
Dog whisperer	*Fathom your companion canine's innermost needs, desires, and anxieties.*
Dog therapist	*Help your canine companion to achieve needs as revealed by dog whisperer.*

VETTING YOUR NANNY

It's a given that your children's nannies (one per child) will be English, wear uniforms, and push extravagant, oversize prams. Still, it's wise to check the background of even the most aesthetically pleasing governess. The United Kingdom's Criminal Records Bureau (CRB) is the first place to turn for information. According to the director of the CRB, "the role of the Criminal Records Bureau is to reduce the risk of abuse by ensuring that those who are unsuitable are not able to work with children and vulnerable adults."

HELPFUL HOUSEHOLD PHRASES FOR SPANISH-SPEAKING EMPLOYEES

Buenos días.
Good day.

Buenas tardes.
Good afternoon.

Buenas noches.
Good evening.

Hola. Estoy muy borracho.
Hi. I'm really drunk.

Esto no está limpio.
This isn't clean.

Hola. Quisiera introducirte a mi nueva/nuevo novia/novio/piscinero. No nos disturbe, por favor.
Hi. I'd like to introduce you to my new girlfriend/boyfriend/pool boy. Please don't disturb us.

Te pareces caliente.
You look hot.

Apurate, muchacha/muchacho.
Hurry up, girl/boy.

Yo sé que es duro vivir sin dinero.
I understand how difficult it is to live with not much money.

No te daré más. Hay otros que quisieran tu trabajo.
I won't give you more. There are others who would like your job.

¿Te incomodarías si nado desnudo?
Will it bother you if I swim naked?

Pues, busca otro trabajo.
Then look for another job.

SEXUAL HARASSMENT

Any responsible star will try to protect staff members from sexual harassment by establishing a uniform code of conduct. Of course, many stars have hung themselves by their own petard by forgetting that such conduct also applies to themselves. If you are going to "fall in love" with an employee, don't begin the affair by informing your love interest of his or her rights.

The International Guild of Professional Butlers offers this sexual harassment policy as an example of how you may inform the rest of your staff of its rights and obligations in this arena:

> NOTE: This is a sample sexual harassment policy, notifying workers that sexual harassment will not be tolerated. Include this form in an Employee Handbook or make it available separately.

In order to provide a productive and pleasant working environment, it is important that we at (_____ Household) endeavor to maintain a workplace characterized by mutual respect. Accordingly, sexual harassment in our workplace will not be tolerated.

Prohibited Activities

Sexual harassment has been defined as a form of sex discrimination, consisting of unwanted sexual advances. Examples of prohibited sexual harassment include:

> *Supervisors or managers explicitly or implicitly suggesting sex in return for a hiring, compensation, promotion, or retention decision.*

> *Verbal or written sexually suggestive or obscene comments, jokes, or propositions.*

> *Unwanted physical contact, such as touching, grabbing, or pinching.*

> *Displaying sexually suggestive objects, pictures, or magazines.*

> *Continual expression of sexual or social interest after an indication that such interest is not desired.*

> *Conduct with sexual implications when such conduct interferes with the employee's work performance or creates an intimidating work environment.*

> *Suggesting or implying that failure to accept a request for a date or sex would adversely affect the employee in respect to a performance evaluation or promotion.*

STAR QUESTION: Is It True What They Say About Pool Technicians?

Yes. Many pool technicians in the Los Feliz to Malibu corridor enjoy fulfilling clients' non-natatorial desires. The lonely star is the one who doesn't ask.

STAR ISSUE: PSYOPS, or Nonlethal Methods for Coping with Driveway Tourists

Even if you opt for a low-key personal life, fans eventually will gather at your gate, hoping to glimpse, touch, or, in difficult cases, assassinate you. Military forces around the world have effectively used psychological operations (PSYOPS) since the time of Jehoshaphat, whose army sang its way to a weaponless victory. More recently, the U.S. military used PSYOPS to dislodge General Manuel Noriega in Panama and to disorient insurgents in Iraq. PSYOPS works just as effectively to neutralize your driveway tourists.

Psychological operations to consider:

Indifference: Ignore the hordes in your driveway. (Difficult when they are blocking your entrance or exit.) Eventually they will leave.

Friendly: Invite them in for tea. (Not advised, for security reasons.) They will become disillusioned by the fact that you, too, have to wash your teacups (or at least have to tell someone to wash them) and will leave.

Icy cordiality: Offer autographs through the gate. (Don't let them grab your hands.) But smile coldly. They will become uncomfortable and leave.

Insecure: Bake the organic, sugar- and wheat-free cookies you favor and distribute them at the gate. They will spit them out and leave.

Hostile: Turn on your curbside sprinkler via remote control before entering or leaving the gate. (Beware: Some people will interpret this as an affectionate gesture.)

Aggressive: Hire armed and insensitive curbside patrols.

Last resort: Play loud classical music and distribute literary novels. Display your plastic surgery scars. Fart with indiscretion, as though you were one of the regular people (RP).

SIX SIGNS OF A STALKER

Stars are pungent stalker bait. If you suspect that someone is stalking you, hire security, notify the police, and pack heat. Here are some signs that you are being stalked.

1. You receive repeated phone calls from the same (sometimes unknown) person, even when you've told them not to contact you again.
2. The person waits for you at your house, at the studio, or at the Ivy.
3. The person makes threats, professes love, or writes hostile reviews of your movies.
4. The person manipulates you by threatening to commit suicide unless you contact them.
5. The person sends you letters and gifts (often with overly romantic or fearsome content).
6. The person lies to others about your behavior and spreads rumors that you are a drug user.

THE STALKER PERSONALITY

According to experts at the Florida International University Victims Advocacy Center, stalkers generally are:

Jealous

Narcissistic

Obsessive-compulsive

Quick to fall in love

Manipulative

Controlling

Awkward and uncomfortable in social situations

Perpetual "victims"

Unable to take no for an answer

Easily moved from rage to love and back again

Unaware of the difference between fantasy and reality

Prone to feel entitled (e.g., "You owe me . . .")

Unable to cope with rejection

Dependent on others for a sense of "self"

Quick to blame others

Smart

LICENSE TO CARRY

All good intentions aside, sometimes your film promotion efforts will unduly excite one or more superfans (SFs). These SFs tend to believe that they have a special relationship with you. If this imaginary relationship sours, they get upset. Even if you have bodyguards, it's still important to be able to defend yourself. In California, people wanting a license to carry a concealed weapon must fill out an application, which is available at the county sheriff's office. According to state law, the sheriff may issue a license to an applicant who is "of good moral character" and who has "good cause" for the license; this license will be valid statewide. In New York, you must apply to the Licensing Division of the New York Police Department, presenting an application that you've downloaded from the Web. In time, you will be interviewed and evaluated. Sadly, it's almost impossible to get approval in either city to carry a concealed weapon, making it very difficult for a star to legally protect him- or herself from obsessed predatory fans (OPFs). Your connections and fame might help you get a permit, but it's doubtful. Furthermore, New York City and Los Angeles, the two locales where you'll most want to protect yourself, don't honor each other's licenses. And neither city will issue a concealed weapons permit to a nonresident. It's a tough world. Stars who want to pack heat will have to do it on the sly, just like the people they fear.

STAR QUESTION: How Do I Coordinate My Gun with My Wardrobe?

Beretta offers stars the opportunity to exercise their creativity and individuality by customizing the look and feel of their personal defense system. The sleek U22 Neos (Greek for "new"), for example, is a lightweight single-action .22 caliber pistol suitable for low-level defensive measures that can be customized to meet your fashion needs. Beretta's interactive website (www.berettausa.com/promotion/U22/neos_land.htm) lets stars choose from a variety of neon grips, sights, barrel configurations, scopes,

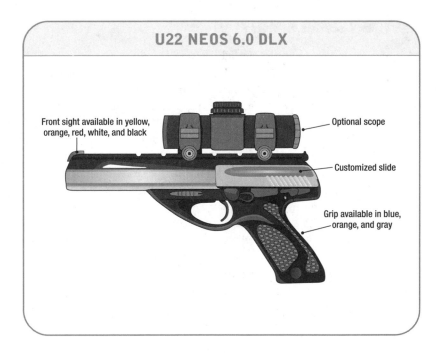

U22 NEOS 6.0 DLX

Front sight available in yellow, orange, red, white, and black

Optional scope

Customized slide

Grip available in blue, orange, and gray

and even carbine kits to make a unique weapon that fits the individual's personality and wardrobe.

DEFENSIVE CLOTHING

Often, concealed weapons have sharp edges that can be uncomfortable. The StreetMaster Covert Operations Shirt is a stylish and comfortable way to carry protective firearms. The shirt has two concealed gun/pepper-spray pockets and two smaller cuff pockets for bullets, a knife, Xanax tablets, or all of the above. Available in black only, this antistalker shirt will blend right in at most Hollywood gatherings.

STREETMASTER SHIRT

Holster pocket (mace)

Holster pocket (pistol)

Cuff pocket (handcuff keys)

Cuff pocket (mini-knife)

THE ENTOURAGE OR POSSE

Only the most confident or mentally "different" stars travel alone. All others travel with caretakers, employees, and friends. Here's what to call the members of your group, whether you're dragging around an entourage (generally for older stars of both sexes and for younger females) or a posse (favored by younger male stars). Whichever you choose, you are expected to cover their expenses. Be advised: Maintaining too large of an entourage or posse has bankrupted many new stars.

ENTOURAGE, AKA "MY PEOPLE"	POSSE, AKA "CREW"
Security detail	*Backup*
Hair and makeup people	*Beauty team*
Clothes stylist	*Girlfriend*
Escort/companion	*Escort service/shortie*
Best friend	*My boys*
Manager	*Manager*
Home or pad	*Crib*
Dough (money)	*Doughlo (money)*

HOLLYWOOD SECRET: Endow Now

Public schools for your children are out of the question, due to security concerns, poor educational performance, and status considerations. Homeschooling, with qualified tutors from back East, is an option. Still, it's best to open doors by making your first endowment to a prestigious academy of your choice no later than the third trimester of your first pregnancy to ensure that your progeny are well-regarded by the Admissions staff. Cash in a briefcase, a prepaid blueprint for a new wing, a truckload of playground equipment, or an all-expenses-paid luxury retreat for all staff members are suitable first donations. Say yes when asked to read aloud from children's books to raise funds at the Spring Fair. (Be sure to alert your publicist to this prime image-burnishing opportunity.)

PREEMPTIVE BIRTHING

Given the physical effects of delivery and the deadline vagaries of the birth process, many star mothers-to-be now schedule Cesarean deliveries well ahead of time. Delivering this way at eight months, rather than Mother Nature's requested nine months, can prevent unnecessary weight gain and reduce the risk of stretch marks in the all-important belly area. When combined with a tummy tuck, this convenient procedure can leave you looking naturally fit and thin immediately following birth. And since Cesareans allow everything to go according to a plan, you'll be able to get right to work, rather than having to allow time for a potentially late or complicated delivery. Still, keep in mind that no matter how well you plan, nature might not respect your schedule. Be sure that any movie contracts include a fully staffed ambulance always at the ready during your last six weeks of pregnancy.

STAR BIRTH CENTER

Cedars-Sinai Medical Center has deluxe maternity suites, with valet parking for your partner or agent, to help give you a pampered postpartum experience. These two- to three-room suites—with hardwood floors, coordinated drapes and bedding, recessed lights, and comfortable furniture—are big enough for a husband, life partner, baby daddy, or nanny. The rooms include well-stocked refrigerators, a stereo, TV, laptop computer with Internet access, hair dryer, free toiletries, and a soft terry-cloth robe. On arriving, you will get a fruit and muffin basket. After the

Cesarean, expect a private dinner for two served on a linen tablecloth. To reserve a room, call 888-DELUXOB.

PLAYTIME

Luxury playhouses for children can be ordered from Posh Tots (www .poshtots.com). Suggestions include the custom-made Fort Bethesda, which comes complete with a sixteen-foot climbing tower and a working flagpole. Cost: $47,000, not including bark chips for the ground.

STAR PETS AND THEIR MEANINGS

Whether your pet barks or growls, it says a lot about you.

STAR PET	STAR MEANING
Siamese cat	*Sophisticated, powerful*
Horse	*Needy, vain, lonely*
House-trained miniature pony	*Really needy*
Great Dane	*Horny*
Savannah (illegal, half-wild housecat)	*Troublesome*
Mutt	*Well-adjusted*
Lizard	*Insecure about your looks*
Lion	*CGS*
Goldfish	*Free-flowing, content, like to swim*
Pit bull	*Urban mystic*
Potbellied pig	*Adventurous, hygienically relaxed*
Fiddler crab	*Creative*

Rat	*Hiding something*
Chihuahua	*Fun-loving, domineering*
Giant millipedes	*Introspective and serious*
Husky	*Serious, chilly*
Giraffe	*Odd*
Chimp	*Wacko*
Snake	*Horny*
Hamster	*Don't care what people say*

LOST ANIMALS

When a star pet wanders away, the star guardian faces certain publicity issues that RP do not.

- They may be portrayed as irresponsible guardians for allowing their pet to disappear.
- They may be portrayed as uncaring guardians if they do not commit the proper resources to their companion animal's recovery.

To avoid these issues, a star should begin recovery efforts immediately after discovering that a pet has disappeared. The most productive, cost-effective method is to hire an experienced pet detective. This method is also most likely to generate additional positive publicity. Pet detectives, usually self-trained, analyze maps, behavioral characteristics of various animals and breeds, and the guardian's lifestyle in order to deduce the location of lost pets. Carl Washington (www.carlwashington-petdetective.com), a renowned pet detective well known for being both discreet and professional, will work with you over the phone and Internet to find your animal. If that fails, he will bring his small poodle, named CoCo, and his Jack Russell terrier, named Rocky, to track your lost companion animal. Both animals pose well for the camera.

GETTING AROUND

TYPE	COMFORT	SIGNALS THAT YOU . . .	COST
Helicopter	Noisy and dusty	Can't be bothered	$860 per hour
Bicycle	None	Care about your body and the world	$8,500 (titanium)
Stretch limo	Spacious and soft	Can't afford a private chauffeur	$80 per hour
Chauffeured Rolls	Buttery	Are secure with your money	If you have to ask . . .
Ducati	Rumbling	Watch Italian movies	$30,000
Toyota Prius hybrid vehicle	Eco-comfort	Suffer from hybris	$20,975
Ferrari Scaglietti	Very much	Are rich, fast, in control, and probably have kids (four-seater)	$237,850
Mercedes SLR Mclaren	Damn right!	Are compensating (experts believe car hoods are inversely proportionate to penis size)	$465,000

ARMORED VEHICLE

Even RP feel threatened while driving around Los Angeles. If security is a concern, consider buying an armored Cadillac DeVille Protection Series or a Lincoln Town Car Ballistic Protection Series vehicle.

STAR KNOWLEDGE: In the Drive

Most people never consider how their cars relate to their real estate. Most star car collectors keep the bulk of their collection garaged, perhaps in an elevator-accessed concrete vault beneath their home. But there's always at least one car out front waiting to be driven. It should live in harmony with your house, so as not to reduce the impact of your architecture.

And it's not just the appearance of the car, but also the idea behind the car, that counts. For instance, no matter how charming it seems, an exquisitely restored 1963 Mercedes-Benz Type W121 190b Binz wagon would look cutely pretentious parked in the drive of a minimalist canyon fantasy (although it might fit beautifully with a rose-covered Tudor). And while a red Ferrari F430 would radiate a discomforting egocentric vibe in front of a vintage Lautner house, it might be perfect resting on the landing pad of a charmless chrome and stucco Malibu cottage. But making an aesthetic match between car and home can be tricky. For professional help, turn to Steven Harris, of Steven Harris Architects in New York. Harris is one of the few well-known architects who, in addition to designing buildings, specializes in advising clients about which cars to keep at their houses. Harris, an expert in the sociology and psychology of who drives what, has paired a '71 Mercedes convertible with a clean '60s modernist house, a little Aston Martin with a shingled bachelor fantasy, and a vintage Land Rover with a country farmhouse, among other combinations. "The caricature of the estate with the Bentleys and the convertible is kind of vulgar," says Harris. "A car tells a lot about you and your ambitions."

HOW TO HIRE A DRIVER

In a world climate where terrorism and kidnapping are the norm, it's wise for stars to avoid the extreme ostentation of stretch limousines and hired cars whenever possible—especially when the studio isn't paying for it. Your own car, whether it's a Bentley or a Prius, will serve you better. However, stars' feet aren't meant to touch pedals. Other than on special occasions and for recreational purposes, you will always be driven. Given your itinerant lifestyle, a full-time driver based in your home might not be the most practical choice. Instead, contract with a chauffeur depot, such as WeDriveU (www.wedriveu.com), that sends someone to drive your car for you. The drivers are road-tested by police officers, carry their own automobile liability insurance, and are trained to keep their eyes on the road, not the backseat. The company will arrange for drivers to meet you at any location in the world.

HOLLYWOOD SECRET:
Service Station to the Stars

Hollywood stars tend to use the two service stations at the following locations, which are noted for their convenience and hospitality toward stars: 9448 West Pico Boulevard and 9988 Wilshire Boulevard.

EARTHQUAKE RISK

Southern California sometimes experiences several hundred small earthquakes a week. Take the following steps to prepare yourself for the day the chandeliers shake: Bolt bookcases to the wall so that your Oscars won't topple; be sure that bedroom mirrors are securely bolted to the ceiling; keep medicine cabinets latched to avoid prescription (and recreational drug) loss; leave denim clothing on open shelves to take advantage of an earthquake's natural tendency to distress fabric.

Also, consider the safety of your less-capable companions during an earthquake. The Federal Emergency Management Agency (FEMA) offers the following suggestions for dealing with pets during just such a disaster:

- Since pets easily become disoriented in an earthquake, they should be identified with tags, leg bands, tattoos, or implanted microchips for easy identification should they get lost. Include the phone number of a friend or relative outside the Los Angeles area.

- Develop an earthquake pet disaster plan, and rehearse it with your family.

- Familiarize your pet with its transport crate, in case you need to evacuate suddenly.

- Practice catching your cat. This can be difficult.

- Make a disaster kit ahead of time for each animal: include leashes, harnesses, muzzles, saddles, toys, blankets, drinking water, food, treats, can openers, medication, chew toys, treadmills, vitamins, grooming supplies, and breath fresheners.

- Pack a first-aid kit, including clippers, tweezers, and antiseptic.

- Purchase a generator to maintain power to heat birds, lizards, and other fragile animals.

- Prepare to move exotic pets, such as lions, to separate areas so as not to endanger rescue personnel.
- After disaster strikes, consider getting professional counseling for your pet.

STAR QUESTION: Where Can I Buy a Richter Scale?

You can't. The Richter scale is a mathematical formula that bears no relation to the electronic device on your bathroom floor.

♦♦♦

CHAPTER 2

SOCIAL LIFE HOW TO STAY CENTERED WHEN EVERYONE ENVIES YOU

PEERS, PESTS, AND OTHER PERSONALITIES

Despite appearances, as a star, you remain human. You have feelings toward others and have desires that beg to be fulfilled. You blush, giggle, and get shy, and you are blustery, vain, and domineering in much the same way you were before you ascended to stardom. But you will soon discover that your quest to satisfy the more basic human needs—friendship, companionship, hot sex—is constantly shadowed by your supernova career. Maintaining a normal social life becomes a job in itself.

A number of issues dominate a star's social contract with his or her peers and underlings, but money and power will be the two most disruptive forces in your life. Your charisma and cash will draw people to you at the same time they drive others away. Those who are caught in your orbit may begin to feel whiplashed by these twin forces, and as a result, your humanity will constantly be challenged by various forms of envious behavior. You may have worked hard to get where you are—or perhaps you are just lucky—but others will be working just as hard to get what you have. Maintaining a normal social life will be impossible—at least as you know it now.

ENTERTAINING AT HOME

Nothing beats a home-cooked meal for making guests feel comfortable, even if you don't cook it yourself. Some tips for a memorable party:

Types of Chefs

- A personal chef will shop, cook, and even clean (when maids are not present) on an as-requested basis for $30 to $125 per hour. While these chefs are, effectively, "temps" and thus don't confer great status on your household, a 25 percent "white-lie" gratuity should ensure that your chef won't reveal his or her temp status to your guests. (Note: Since personal chefs work for a variety of clients, there's always the risk that one of your guests will recognize your chef from another star household.)

- A private chef works for you alone and is the ultimate status symbol. Expect to pay upward of $65,000 a year, plus benefits and housing, for a chef with up to ten years' experience; one with up to twenty years' experience could cost as much as $150,000. Private floating chefs are also available, as follows: $65,000 for yachts up to 140 feet; $90,000 for yachts up to 200 feet; whatever the market will bear for yachts 200 feet and more. There will be additional charges for shopping by helicopter from far out at sea. Expect to pay the chef's talent agency 10–15 percent of the annual fee on top of the salary.

THE PRICE OF GOSSIP

Star parties are petri dishes for the celebrity gossip that fills TV shows and magazines. It is the host's responsibility to contain any bacterial growth by requiring employees to sign confidentiality agreements. It's best to specify exactly what employees risk by leaking gossip to the press. The following provisions, from a well-known Hollywood couple's staff agreement, are a good example of how to outline the exact costs of indiscretion:

Employee acknowledges that _____ are internationally well-known figures who will be seriously harmed both professionally and personally by the unauthorized disclosure of Confidential Information, with the amount of such harm likely to be very substantial and to vary with the type and extent of disclosure and that it would be difficult and impractical to measure the full extent of the actual damages caused by Employee's violation of this agreement. Accordingly, the parties agree upon the following schedule of liquidated damages:

a. Private disclosure or repetition of Confidential Information, $50,000 for each person to whom each such disclosure or repetition is made.

b. Causing, participating in, or cooperating in, aiding or abetting publication, broadcast, or other public disclosure or repetition of Confidential Information:

1) In a newspaper or magazine, $20 for each copy printed, with a minimum of $1,000,000 per publication

2) In a book, $250 for each copy printed, with a minimum of $1,000,000 for publication in the United States, $500,000 per territory for publication in Japan, U.K., Germany, Italy, France, Canada, Australia, Scandinavia, or Spain, and $250,000 per publication in other countries

3) By theatrical exhibition, $20,000 per showing

4) In a U.S. network television broadcast, $5,000,000 per broadcast

5) In a U.S. non-network television broadcast, $2,000,000 per broadcast

6) In a foreign television broadcast (a) in major territories, $1,000,000 per broadcast; (b) in other foreign television broadcasts, $500,000 per broadcast

7) In video cassettes, discs, or other video devices, $30 for each unit manufactured, with a minimum of $1,000,000

8) On audio records (tape, disc, or otherwise), $10 for each unit manufactured with a minimum of $1,000,000

9) By other public disclosure or repetition, $1,000,000 for each such disclosure or repetition

c. With respect to the first time, unintentional disclosure of Confidential Information, only one-half of the sums specified above shall be payable.

GUEST FORMULA FOR A GREAT DINNER PARTY

Great dinner parties (GDPs) are like good lawns. They need to be seeded with the proper blend of mixed creative bohemians (MCBs); industry players (IPs); sharklike agents (SAs); financial services moguls (FSMs); intellectual directors (IDs); reformed gang members or addicts (RGMAs); innocent, ambitious, recent arrivals from the Midwest (IARAMs); male or female porn stars (MFPSs); Ivy League eggheads (ILEs); pretty and heavily accented foreigners (PHAFs); and board riders (BRs).

The formula followed by successful star hosts is:

50% star + 15% MCB + 2.5% IP + 2.5% SA + 5% FSM + 5% ID + 5% RGMA + 5% IARAM + 5% MFPS + 2% ILE + 2% PHAF + 1% BR = GDP

GREAT DINNER PARTY GUEST DENSITY

To achieve maximal GDPGD, it's wise to follow airline industry protocol and overbook invited guests (IGs). Assume a no-show (NS) rate of 25 percent; most of these will be star invitees (SIs) who do not need the affirmative powers of your invitation, unlike lesser invitees (LIs). Therefore, the correct invitation equation for a dinner party (DP) of twelve IGs, including six SIs, is:

6 LIs + 8 SIs = 14 IGs − 25% NSSI (2) = 12 IGs (6 LIs + 6 SIs)

If you experience a last-minute shortage (LMS) of SIs, turn to Al Lampkin Entertainment, 1817 West Verdugo Avenue, Burbank, California 91506, 818-846-4951 (www.allampkin.com). For a reasonable fee, this venerable agency will send star look-alikes (SLALs) to mingle with your LIs and make small talk about upcoming projects. None of your LIs will suspect a thing, because the thought that a star would resort to SLALs to counter an LMS of SIs is too far-fetched.

IDEAL DP IG SEATING CHART

SIs are often better looking than LIs. But LIs often have more interesting things to say. The savvy star host will alternate SIs with LIs, seat by seat. In the past, star hosts needed to concern themselves with seating by gender as well as by status. However, in modern Hollywood, sexual orientation is less rigid (and often hidden), and a host who seats according to

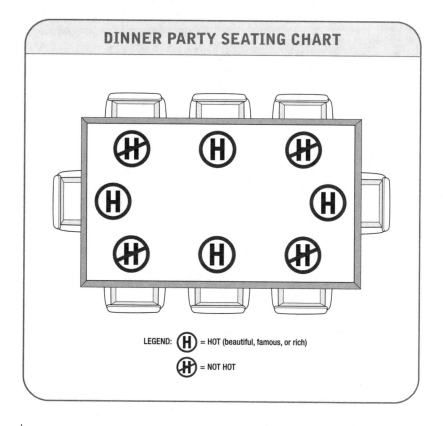

gender risks making a damaging social gaffe. To be safe, seat according to this foolproof formula: Alternate according to who's hot and who's not, rather than by gender.

DINNER TABLE CONVERSATION

The host will try to guide the dinner table conversation according to the following subjects:

ACCEPTABLE TOPICS	TOPICS TO AVOID
Sports	Steroids
Literature	Screenwriters
Food	Food poisoning
Sunspots	Liver spots
Good help is hard to find	Your staff's contact info
LA and NYC	The in-between
Childhood	Your children
Plastic surgery	The prevalence of breast implants at the party

STAR KNOWLEDGE: The All-Purpose Menu

Since a typical dinner party includes fishitarians, anorexics, raw foodists, and breatharians, it can be difficult to create a menu that will accommodate everyone's food needs, preoccupations, and desires. But the cuisine of the Mongols, a nomadic tribe that once ruled from Vienna to Beijing, can be adapted to fit any star party. It will allow your staff to answer "no problem" when their people call your people to outline food phobias. Of course, the Mongols had different lifestyle demands than those found in present-day Hollywood. At night these nomads would tether their horses and gather around the fire to spear meat and vegetables and dip them in pots of boiling oil. Update this idea by having your cook prepare platters of sliced or cubed vegetables, beef, chicken, and fish. Fill Mongolian hot pots with oil or broth and heat them with a Sterno at the table. Let your guests spear the foods that fit their dietary needs and stick them in the pots. Put some garlic bread in a basket for old-fashioned eaters. Tell the raw foodists to nibble the uncooked vegetables. Breatharians can step outside for a smoke.

PROCLIVITIES AND PROPENSITIES

Generally, Hollywood people are accustomed to doing whatever they want, whenever they want. A star host's tolerance levels should be based on the guest's status and influence. For instance, open cocaine use by a studio head isn't cause for alarm; but blatant nicotine consumption by a character actor need not be tolerated. Sensitive hosts maintain at least one "coatroom" where guests can indulge in sexual encounters and consume entertaining substances away from prying eyes (unless they like to be seen, in which case a glass-walled pool house can serve to great effect).

SWAG

Youth is highly valued in Hollywood, and it's a rare industry titan who hesitates to honor his or her inner child. This explains why most stars and hangers-on are so captivated by gift baskets, the grown-up version of the party bags given out at children's birthday parties. While gift baskets have long been a staple of award ceremonies, stars in the know are aware that promotional companies will also create gift baskets for private parties with a high celebrity quotient. Your baskets should include products with prestige, class, and value such as a diving watch, a certificate for a spa retreat, round-trip tickets to Bhutan, or a catered picnic on Mount Saint Helens. But you need not purchase any items yourself—let big corporations pay for all the gifts you hand out. Have your party planner contact a marketing company that specializes in placing gift bags—Distinctive Assets (www.distinctiveassets.com) or Backstage Creations (www.backstagecreations.com)—and they'll take care of all the details. After you have catered to their inner child, your guests will leave your party happy, their baskets of swag bouncing up and down in the backseat of the Bentley.

DOG RUN SOCIALIZING

It is difficult for stars to mingle with regular people (RP) in a natural way. The star always suspects that the regular person is kissing up, and the regular person always suspects the star is looking down. However, dog runs have a singular way of democratizing relationships. Most dogs, including big stars like Lassie, aren't snobs. Your dog might introduce you to another star or even to a nonstar with a really cool dog. Two runs in particular are comfortable for stars.

Laurel Canyon Park: A yellow sign at the entrance to this dog run off Mulholland Drive reads, "Caution—Mountain Lions." But this one-acre grassy run, replete with swimming pools for the dogs and shaded benches where stars can shoot the breeze, is nonetheless a relaxed place. There is even a fenced-off area for "small or timid dogs only."

Runyon Canyon: There are always a number of stars walking their dogs up the steep canyons of this Hollywood park located at the top of North Fuller Avenue. The best trail veers left uphill about a hundred yards into the park and loops up to Mulholland and back down the other side of the canyon to the park entrance.

CANINE COITUS

While unprotected sexual activity is rampant in most Hollywood area dog runs, you needn't be concerned about canine STDs. Section 53.30 of the Los Angeles Municipal Code, which is posted at all dog runs, states,

"Dogs with communicable diseases are not allowed on park premises at any time."

STAR ISSUE: Dating a Nobody

Yes, stars have dated (and even married!) both cinematographers and small-time country music singers. Generally not at the same time, although that could make for great PR during a career slump. Please note, however, that dating a nonstar brings up a number of difficult issues. On the plus side, the sexual attraction necessary to pull you to a nobody in the first place probably guarantees that you won't become a DIZO couple. On the negative side, nobodies tend to become star helicopters (mates that always hover about). When considering a relationship with a nonstar, you must weigh what you bring to the table against what the nobody brings. This chart will help even the most lust-blinded star:

THE TABLE

THE STAR BRINGS	THE NONSTAR BRINGS
Over-the-top lifestyle	Nine-to-five workday
Power	Desire for power
Money	Good credit rating (hopefully)
Glamour	Attractiveness
Big house	Big mortgage
PR team	Favorite sports team
Snob appeal	Sex appeal
Fabulous acquaintances	Friends
Accountant	H&R Block electronic refund
Manager/agent	Quicken
Therapist	Priest

SATISFYING SHORT-TERM SEXUAL URGES

The men's stalls in the Spanish Colonial–style bathrooms of Will Rogers Memorial Park at 9650 Sunset Boulevard, across from the Beverly Hills Hotel, have served many major celebrities well. As have the sex workers trolling Sunset Boulevard in Hollywood. However, the unpredictable nature of undercover LAPD vice officers makes it difficult to determine when and where such encounters are safe. A messy arrest could lead to a PR nightmare. Best to do your research before going out to "gronge." The experts at www.worldsexguide.org post daily updates on safe Los Angeles venues for encountering street prostitutes, full-service massage parlors, and male and female pickup spots. Reviews of world travel destinations are also available.

HOLLYWOOD SECRET: Hooking Up with Fellow Stars or Industry Players

As a star, you figure in the fantasy lives of everyone on the planet, including those of fellow stars. One thin, blonde star has a surefire method for fulfilling her own fantasies: She has a trusted aide tell the object of her sexual desire that he may meet her at a certain hotel on a specific night for a specified number of hours. The aide makes it clear that this is a one-time, nonromantic encounter. Confidentiality is reasonably assured, as the object of desire won't want to sabotage his chances of being invited back at a later date. Sometimes a star's life will be so focused on work and image that she doesn't get the time to choose her own conquests. In this case, the star should outline her preferences— age, coloring, body type, "size," etc.—to her agent, and let him take care of the rest.

ENGAGEMENT: Traditional Values Predominate

Hollywood remains a largely 1950s society, where men earn more than women and tend to date and marry down a generation or two—

sometimes three. Whether industry executives or stars, these men generally seek heavily fortified breasts, muscular midsections, beautiful wardrobes, and unlined faces, along with killer personalities. Faced with such Neanderthals, the female star, no matter how successful, is entitled to her own retro behavior. When a Hollywood man asks a Hollywood star what kind of engagement ring she'd like, she should reply, "Make it hurt," and pat his wallet pocket.

BUYING RINGS

According to the American Gem Society, diamonds are judged according to the four Cs:

- Cut. The cut of the diamond is the most critical aspect in determining its value. Modern diamonds are cut to emphasize "fire" rather than carat weight, which was more important to previous generations.

- Color. Diamonds are graded according to color on a spectrum ranging from clear (most valuable) to yellow (least valuable).

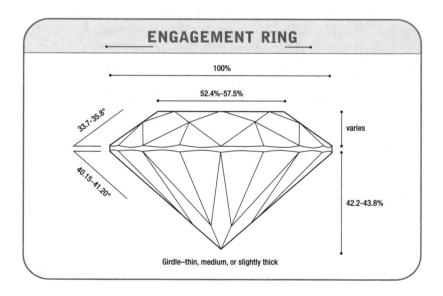

ENGAGEMENT RING

100%

52.4%-57.5%

33.7-35.8°

40.15-41.20°

varies

42.2-43.8%

Girdle—thin, medium, or slightly thick

- Clarity. The most valuable diamonds have no "crystal" or "feather" inclusions when viewed through a microscope.
- Carats. This is a measurement of weight. The cost of carats increases geometrically. A one-carat diamond might cost five times as much as a half-carat diamond. And weight is not the only determining factor. There are three-carat diamonds that cost more than some four-carat diamonds, due to other C factors.

Diamonds are also judged by a fifth C:

- Conflict. According to the United Nations, the profits of many diamonds sold in the world market are used to finance armies in countries such as Sierra Leone that rape, mutilate, and annihilate civilians. Some experts believe Osama Bin Laden uses diamond money to finance his operations. To avoid wearing a "blood diamond," check with the Jewelers for Clean Diamond Imports for a list of approved retailers.

STAR KNOWLEDGE: How to Suggest a Prenup

Prenup negotiations are among the most difficult conversations your attorney will have with your intended. To make matters easier, you should e-mail your fiancé(e) a list of your reasons for seeking a prenup before you send over your attorney. Here are some tips for opening this conversation, based on information from the Equality in Marriage Institute:

- Don't drop this bomb a week before the wedding; bring it up well in advance.
- Have this conversation with your loved one in a place where you normally have serious conversations—that's why e-mail is perfect.
- Discuss the subject in a calm, caring fashion.
- Say that you intend for the marriage to last forever but that you want to protect yourself just in case it doesn't.
- Allow your betrothed to believe that he or she has some say in the wording of the document.

Once your intended has agreed to the idea of a prenup, pass the matter on to your lawyer and be done with it. This subject should never be discussed in bed.

THE WEDDING

A Hollywood marriage can serve two distinct and equally noble purposes:

- Love's fulfillment
- Career's advancement

The wedding is key to determining how these factors will be combined, if at all. There are four types of weddings available to you:

False: The false wedding takes place between a star and the one who has smitten him or her but without the benefit of a marriage license, blood test, or prenup. These ceremonies most often follow a days-long celebratory binge by the romantic couple and usually terminate shortly after the kiss. Fortunately for the star, since nothing is legal, nothing will be lost in the transaction. These weddings normally take place in Las Vegas without benefit of a celebrity-wedding planner or Breathalyzer.

Assuming you have thought about marriage for longer than it takes to dispatch six kir royales and a pack of Marlboro Lights and have completed all prenuptial and contractual requirements as per legal counsel, you may proceed with one of three types of genuine weddings:

Quiet and Romantic: Have your lawyer draw up a confidentiality agreement for your wedding planner, instructing him or her to use secure computer networks, in-office shredders, and bug-detecting devices when working on your wedding. All your transactions with the wedding planner will be done through a mediary, and your and your intended's names will not be revealed until the day of the ceremony. The invitation will not list the wedding location. Instead, it will say, "You will be contacted at a later date with location information." The invitations will be delivered by private security guards just two weeks or less in advance of the date. You cannot have a private wedding with a crowd, so limit yourself to fifty guests. Invite only close friends and family, and do not consider business advancement or networking potential when making your guest list. The ceremony must take place on a deserted island or in a private home, preferably in another country. Be prepared to cancel the ceremony at the last minute if the press gets wind of it. You will not profit in any way from the wedding, but you might remain in love.

Loud and Exploitative: These weddings, with helicopters full of paparazzi flying overhead and crowds charging the front entrance, are good for a star in need of a career boost or for "lavender" weddings, where a star is getting married as a cover for his or her homosexuality. The star maintains the fiction of not wanting publicity but doesn't hesitate to answer any and all queries from *InStyle* magazine regarding the ceremony. Key magazine and newspaper columnists will be invited as "friends" of the bride and groom. Your production company will film the ceremony for the press release. All expenses, from the ten thousand roses decorating the podium to the $10,000 gift bags given to each guest, will be sponsored by various corporations eager to be associated with your good name.

Quiet and Exploitative: Like the quiet and romantic wedding in every detail except one: You charge a magazine an extravagant sum (to be negotiated by your PR agent) to document, publicize, and analyze every detail of the ceremony after it takes place.

SELF-ESTEEM INDEX

Some star weddings affect the zeitgeist (a German word meaning "spirit of the time, or the moral and intellectual currents of an era"), some don't. Two important online services will help you track how important your wedding is to the public at large.

The websites www.oddschecker.com and www.bodog.com offer betting odds on sports events and life occurrences. If odds are being offered regarding the duration of your marriage, you've had an effect. It doesn't matter how good or bad the odds are. What matters is that your nuptials have been noticed.

The website www.google.com/press/zeitgeist.html lists the most popular search queries of the week. Equally noted side by side are the ten queries on the rise and the ten that are descending. It also offers a list of the most requested images online. Find your name and see what effect your nuptials are having on the world.

WEDDING MECHANICS

Star weddings have certain elements not found in civilian ceremonies:

- Decoy brides, deployed as necessary to confuse journalists
- Private planes filled with first-class seating to ferry guests to the ceremony
- Antipaparazzi perimeter patrols
- Gift bags filled with watches, vacations, and jewelry from corporate sponsors
- Secret passwords for all invitees
- VIP rooms for select guests
- Copyrighted I dos

STAR ISSUE: Homemade Sex Tapes

Like many Americans, some stars enjoy cameras even when they're not on set. Unfortunately, modern technology allows homemade sex tapes or digital images to be quickly copied and distributed. Obviously, computer hard drives and videocassettes can be stolen and the images instantly made available via the Internet, so frisky stars should take proper security precautions. However, it's little known that thieves can now steal images of your sexual practices without even entering your house. An increasing number of hackers "wardrive" celebrity neighborhoods, cruising the streets of Beverly Hills and other star locales with electronic devices that alert them to wireless computer networks and even wireless cameras installed in local bedrooms. These hackers can access a star's computer network or just record the images being captured on a wireless camera as stars huff and puff in bed. There is nothing wrong with filming sex between two (or more) consenting adults. At times, these intimate homemade videos help improve a marriage or relationship. However, since your sex acts may be broadcast, be sure to look your best and act your sexiest whenever the cameras are on. And if you want privacy, hire a cybersecurity expert to put up some walls between your bedroom and the outside world.

THE SEX SET

The loveliest homemade porn is filmed at home, in a clean, orderly bedroom with muted light filtering in through the windows. If you are using a stationary camera, be prepared to stop action midact to reframe the shot. You can avoid these disruptions by hiring a professional camera operator to film your act, but be sure to check with your partner first. Some people are uncomfortable being watched. Whichever method you choose, use indirect lighting, such as globe lamps or candles, to conceal any unsightly body parts that haven't yet been surgically corrected. And always be conscious of the angle of the dangle. Occasionally a star will respond to career softening or insecurity by engineering the release of a sex session, either on tape or over the Internet. While this stunt often boosts the careers of B celebrities, it always has the reverse effect on true stars. Avoid this temptation at all costs. Enjoy your homemade porn among the company of good friends. And never give them a copy.

STAR QUESTION: Who Is My Friend?

REAL FRIENDS	STAR****ER FRIENDS
Call before dropping by	*Never leave*
Don't talk about your work	*Want to know every detail*
Tell you when you've put on weight	*Say you look great*
Don't borrow money	*Don't borrow money (because they expect you to just give it to them)*
Like your mom	*Hate your family*
Get mad at you on occasion	*Offer nothing but praise*

Jump out and fill up the gas tank	*Moan about self-serve pumps*
Call every now and then	*Have you on speed dial*
Encourage you to cut back on caffeine	*Borrow your Starbucks card*
Offer to watch your kids	*Talk down to your nanny*
Proudly tell their other friends that they know you	*Tattoo your initials on their neck*

SUPPORTIVE FRIENDS OR FRIENDS YOU SUPPORT?

REASONABLE EXPENSE	DO NOT PAY
Baby shower gift for their firstborn	*Their overdue child-support payments*
Dinner out	*Breakfast, lunch, dinner, and snacks out*
Coffee with milk	*Quadruple venti caramel no-fat soy, no-whip Frappuccino*
Ginseng-up	*Viagra bill*
Promotional T-shirt from your new movie	*Afternoon spree at Versace*
Limo out to the house in Malibu	*Private jet to your yacht in Monte Carlo*
New swimsuit	*New swimming pool*
Sunblock at the beach	*Botox injections*

♦♦♦

CHAPTER 3

SELF IMPROVING YOUR MIND AND BODY GOES WITH THE JOB

CONTROLLING YOUR REFLECTION

The process of becoming a star is transformative in ways that RP could never understand. You work and compromise and work some more; then you wake up following your first really big premiere only to realize that you are living in a different universe from the one you used to occupy. In the process of becoming a star, many actors fear losing touch with their "true" selves. Yet loss of self can be the beginning of something great. Heralded mystics, such as St. John the Divine and Buddha, and globally influential politicians, such as Gandhi and Bill Clinton, were all transformed by personal experiences that destroyed their sense of self and led them to start anew. In your case, the naive, ambitious young person who first crossed the border of Hollywood and Vine may not be the same self who now bunks in a glass-walled Richard Meier home and takes meetings with industry players (IPs) poolside at the Bel-Air. But let's be honest: Your left profile is probably a lot better for it. As your personality and bone structure evolve, you improve. And always remember, as a public role model, becoming more than you really are is nothing if not a patriotic act. Primal-scream therapy, surgery, exercise, cosmetics, full-time life coaches, and other self-improvement expenses are legitimate tax write-offs.

STAR POWER

That sense of inner strength and superiority that flows through your body, energizing every cell and thought even when you are feeling down and neglected, is technically known as "star power" (SP). This mysterious force of nature is rarely found in RP, yet it is a central component of all star bodies. It is what led you to Hollywood in the first place. While, like RP, you may exhibit disturbing mental and physical flaws, they will always be countered by surges of SP. Adoration enhances SP, so as your star rises you'll only become more charismatic, beautiful, and enviable to RP. Don't be afraid to rely on SP when faced with any challenge.

DAILY DIVA AFFIRMATIONS

Some divas, such as Mae West and Elizabeth Taylor, are born, but most are made. To enhance your own divinity, repeat the following affirmations at the prescribed moments, every day, for the rest of your Hollywood life (preferably while standing in front of a full-length mirror).

Upon Waking

I am the queen of my own existence. I serve no one but by many am served.

Following Breakfast (said while smoothing hands over abdomen)

I do not need to eat food in the same way that other people eat food; coffee, fruit, and water will sustain me until the next meal.

Midmorning

As queen of my own existence, I determine my own reality. Lack of protein and carbohydrates will not affect me.

After Lunch

A true star forgives herself for eating chili dogs and French fries for lunch. I will bounce back, without jiggling.

At the Gym

I am better than all these other bitches.

Shopping

It's my money, not my accountant's; I can buy whatever I want.

Cocktail Party

Let them mingle with me; I will not mingle with them.

Dinner

A diva does not eat in front of strangers. A diva pushes food around her plate. A diva is strong.

Dessert

Chocolate mud cake contains skin-toning antioxidants. A double dose has twice the effect.

At the Club

I am the queen of my own existence. All hail me on the dance floor.

In Front of the Mirror at Home

The lighting is so unflattering. I must have it changed.

In Bed

THE DIVANITY PRAYER
God grant me the pomposity
To reject the things I cannot change
The verbiage to force others to change the things they can
And the wisdom to show indifference

TEN COMMON PHYSICAL FLAWS

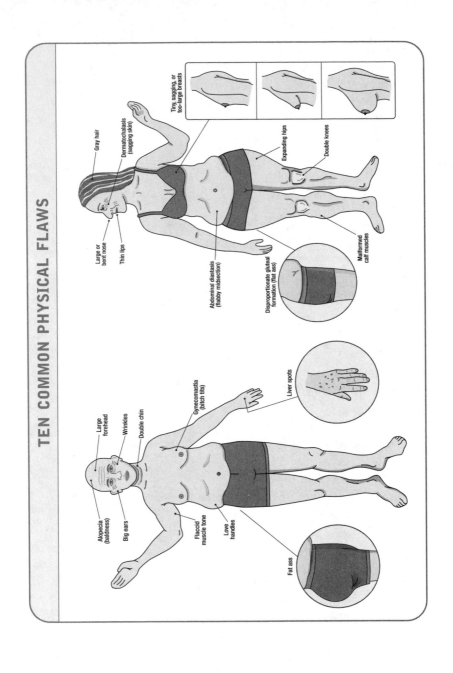

Gray hair

Dermatochalasis (sagging skin)

Large or bent nose

Thin lips

Expanding hips

Double knees

Abdominal diastasis (flabby midsection)

Disproportionate gluteal formation (flat ass)

Malformed calf muscles

Tiny, sagging, or too-large breasts

Large forehead

Wrinkles

Double chin

Gynecomastia (bitch tits)

Liver spots

Alopecia (baldness)

Big ears

Flaccid muscle tone

Love handles

Fat ass

TEN COMMON PHYSICAL FLAWS

Some of these flaws can easily be corrected. Others will be controlled by makeup and wardrobe artists, camera people, and postproduction technologists. Examine yourself so that you're aware of which flaws, if any, might affect your career.

Men

Alopecia (baldness)

Love handles

Flaccid muscle tone

Double chin

Gynecomastia (bitch tits)

Wrinkles

Liver spots

Big ears

Fat ass

Large forehead

Women

Abdominal diastasis (flabby midsection)

Large or bent nose

Disproportionate gluteal formation (flat ass)

Thin lips

Sagging, tiny, or too-large breasts

Expanding hips

Dermatochalasis (sagging skin of the eye)

Malformed calf muscles

Gray hair

Double knees

STAR KNOWLEDGE: Turn Your Ass into an Asset

This is a little-used and risky alternative for anyone frightened of surgery or too lazy to hit the gym. If nature, or gluttony, has endowed you with a particularly large or unattractive body part, take control of your image and make it a cause for celebration. At least one star has beaten the tyranny of Hollywood anorexia by flaunting her large derriere for the cameras and making it her symbol. Numerous male stars have turned their lardy midsections into objects of fascination. A scarred, broken face can be repackaged, with proper public relations techniques, into a mysterious mask of attraction. An underdeveloped bustline can be used, humorously, to draw empathy. Highlighted and flaunted, baldness becomes a symbol of male virility. It's all in the marketing.

PLASTIC SURGERY OPTIONS EXAMINED FOR COST, PROCEDURE, AND RECOVERY: A Look at Some Common Surgeries

Tummy Tuck

Work: Remove excess fat and skin and tighten abdominal-wall muscles

Time: Two to five hours; inpatient or outpatient, depending on circumstances

Cost: $6,000–8,000*

Anesthesia: General or local with sedation

Bad news: Possible temporary pain, swelling, soreness, numbness, bruising, and tiredness lasting several months

*Note: Prices reflect average costs of plastic surgery in the United States, excluding New York City, where costs tend to be 50 percent higher.

Really bad news: Possible blood clots, infection, internal bleeding, and conspicuous scarring, which makes it tough to wear two-button jeans

Back to work: Four to six weeks

Duration of results: Varies; too many pints of Ben and Jerry's can lead to relapse surgery.

Breast Enlargement

Work: Install saline or silicone implants to enlarge breasts

Time: Two to five hours

Cost: $5,000–8,000

Anesthesia: Local with sedation, or general

Bad news: Temporary soreness, swelling, change in nipple sensation, bruising

Really bad news: May need second surgery to remove or replace implants due to deflation, scar tissue, bleeding, or infection. Some women have reported symptoms similar to those of serious immune disorders. Men may tease you on the street. Your husband may ask for upgrades.

Back to work: A few days but can't have physical contact with breasts for three to four weeks. Scars will fade in several months to a year.

Duration of results: Varies. Implants that last into late middle age make women look teenile.

Collagen Injections

Work: Jack up creased or sunken facial skin; plump up lips; soften backs of hands. Works best on thin, dry, light-colored skin. Most people use bovine (cow) collagen. But you may also use harvested collagen (called *autologen*) by having a lab process the leftover skin from your tummy tuck, have collagen cloned (called *isolagen*) from a plug of skin taken from behind your ear, or use collagen from donor corpses (called *dermolagen*). These human-based collagens are said to last longer, though there are no guarantees.

Time: Fifteen minutes to one hour per session. Numerous sessions may be required.

Cost:

> *Bovine: $300–800 per session*
>
> *Autologen: $800–1,000*
>
> *Isolagen: $1,000–1,500*
>
> *Dermolagen: $500–1,000*

Anesthesia: None with collagen; local with fat

Bad news: Possible temporary stinging, throbbing, or burning sensation, faint redness, and excess fullness; trouble slurping soup

Really bad news: Collagen can cause an allergic reaction, swelling, flulike symptoms, autoimmune disease. Fat and collagen injections may also cause infection.

Duration of results: A few months to one year

Facial Implants

Work: Alter the balance and shape of your face by implanting a molded plastic form under the skin that changes the shape of your chin, cheekbones, or jaw.

Time: One half to two hours

Cost: $2,000–6,000

Anesthesia: Local along with sedation, or general

Bad news: Possible numbness, stiffness, and swelling. Implants can slide like a house down a muddy mountainside. Following jaw surgery, you may be unable to open your mouth fully for several weeks (possibly negating need for liposuction).

Really bad news: Possible infection, necessitating removal of implant, or tight scar tissue leading to an unnaturally shaped face

Duration of results: Forever, barring structural avalanche

Hair Replacement

Work: Implant plugs or flaps of hair from elsewhere on body

Time: One to three hours; often requires multiple procedures

Cost: $4,000–20,000

Anesthesia: Local is most common; some flap work requires general.

Bad news: Achy scalp, unnatural look, feelings of shame over the transplanted butt hairs sprouting from head

Really bad news: Infection, scarring, failure to "take"

Duration of results: Forever

Resurfacing of Face

Work: Use CO_2 lasers to smooth away fine wrinkles, soften lines, and minimize scars and discoloring

Time: A few minutes to more than an hour, in a series of multiple sessions

Cost: $4,000–5,000

Anesthesia: Local with sedation, or general

Bad news: Acute sensitivity to sun and makeup, pink or red skin for up to six months

Really bad news: Laser burns, scarring, unusual skin color, viral infections; kids might call out "Freddy!" as you pass

Duration of results: Lasts for years but does not prevent new wrinkles or lines as skin ages

Male Breast Reduction

Work: Get rid of femalelike breasts using liposuction or surgery to remove glandular tissue

Time: At least one hour

Cost: $3,000–6,000

Anesthesia: General or local

Bad news: Bruising, swelling, numbness, burning sensation

Really bad news: Infection, rippled or baggy skin, permanent pigment changes; may lead to vulgar locker room jokes or a need to replace your dress-up lingerie with a smaller size.

Duration of results: Permanent

DETERMINING IF YOU ARE COMPATIBLE WITH YOUR PLASTIC SURGEON

The most forward-thinking stars now request their surgeon's date of birth before scheduling a surgery. Then they pay their astrologist up to

$1,000 to work up a star chart. This chart is then used to determine if the surgeon, the surgery, and the patient are astrologically compatible.

BDD

For some stars, one cosmetic surgery is too many and a thousand wouldn't be enough. If you remain dissatisfied with your body no matter how much dieting, exercise, or surgery you submit to, you might suffer from body dysmorphic disorder (BDD). BDD sufferers are preoccupied with minor or imaginary physical flaws and spend far too much time trying to correct them. The resulting anxiety can cause victims to constantly check their appearance in mirrors, groom themselves to excess, and endlessly seek reassurances from others about their appearance. While these symptoms would seem to apply to almost every star, people with actual BDD can be discerned by the intensity of their preoccupation and by the fact that no amount of complimentary ass-kissing ever makes them feel better. Sadly, even cosmetic surgery fails to help victims of the disease come to terms with their body image, leading some patients to get angry or even violent toward their doctors. This disorder is sometimes successfully treated with medication and cognitive therapy.

COMMON PERSONALITY FLAWS

Most personality flaws stem either from an excess of one trait or a deficit of another. The following disorders, as outlined in the American Psychiatric Association's *Diagnostic and Statistical Manual of Mental Disorders* (fourth edition), are among the most common in Hollywood:

Histrionic Personality Disorder

Symptoms

- Uncomfortable whenever he or she is not the center of attention
- Inappropriate seductive or provocative behavior

- Shallow or seemingly fake emotional displays
- Dramatic, theatrical, and exaggerated emotions
- Easily influenced by others
- Inability to examine unconscious thought patterns

Treatment
- Psychotherapy
- Focus on solutions to short-term problems
- Therapist should take a skeptical approach to the patient's exaggerations (except when they relate to suicidal thoughts)
- Medications are not useful for this disorder

Narcissistic Personality Disorder

Symptoms
- Grandiose behavior or fantasies of success and achievement
- Need for approval and admiration from others
- Lack of empathy for others
- Tendency to exaggerate
- Belief that he or she is special and should only associate with other high-caliber people or institutions
- Takes advantage of others for personal gain
- Envy of others
- Belief that others are envious of him or her
- Arrogance or haughtiness that masks inner low self-esteem

Treatment
- Psychotherapy that encourages empathetic feelings toward others
- Hospitalization

Paranoid Personality Disorder

Symptoms

- A pervasive distrust of others
- Fear of being exploited or harmed
- Preoccupation with the lack of loyalty of others

Treatment

- Psychotherapy that increases coping skills
- Rapport-building with psychotherapist
- Hospitalization
- Medications are generally contraindicated, except for certain antipsychotics if person is severely delusional and tends toward self-harm

STAR ISSUE: Hiring a Life Coach

Sometimes the piecemeal approach to personality improvement fails. In this case, a star might benefit from the more holistic approach to self-improvement offered by a life coach. The following symptoms justify calling in a life coach:

- Crying in bed on bright afternoons
- Feelings of low self-esteem even as your big budget blockbuster takes the world by storm
- Serial sex with people of far lower status
- Temper tantrums, such as throwing phones at hotel desk clerks or punching paparazzi

In order to assess the star's needs, the star life coach usually shadows the star for most of the day, whether at home, on set, at the manicurist, or on dinner dates and then implements a program of change. This program usually involves a combination of psychotherapy, motivational instruction, and an action plan that kicks the star "in the pants." Benefits include:

- More satisfying communication with others
- Increased fulfillment in life
- Less exposure to STDs
- Fewer lonely moments

Life coaches can easily earn $40,000 a month. With a careful strategy and good teamwork, your publicist, business manager, and agent should be able to convince the studio to fold some of these charges into your current film's budget.

With the life coach industry expanding rapidly, many new coaches are hanging up shingles without the requisite experience. Since coaches aren't licensed, it is important to choose a reliable professional. Have your business manager review the credentials of four coaches and then choose two for you to interview. You'll know which one makes you click.

STAR QUESTION: Are You Driven by ADHD?

These days it's common to hear someone say, "Oh, man, I am just so ADHD," when they've drifted off into a daydream or flubbed a task. However, for some stars, attention deficit hyperactivity disorder is not just an excuse for failing to memorize a script; it is a challenging reality. While ADHD kids are often drugged, disciplined, chastised, and ostracized, stars can take a more positive approach to their own neurotransmitter peculiarities. Some ADHD symptoms might actually work to a star's benefit. Common ADHD personality pluses include:

- High intelligence
- Active imagination
- Great (if brief) enthusiasm
- Openness to spontaneity
- Unusual conversational skills

CIGARETTES, HEROIN, OR COFFEE?

During his tenure at the National Institute on Drug Abuse, Jack E. Henningfield, Ph.D., rated some popular and easily obtained Hollywood drugs that are known for their addictive and intoxicating qualities. The scale ranges from 1 (lowest) to 6 (highest). The following chart can help stars determine which avenues of abuse to avoid.

Drug	Dependence	Withdrawal	Tolerance	Reinforcement	Intoxication
Nicotine	6	4	5	3	2
Heroin	5	5	6	5	5
Cocaine	4	3	3	6	4
Alcohol	3	6	4	4	6
Caffeine	2	2	2	1	1
Marijuana	1	1	1	2	3

Explanation of terms:

Dependence refers to how easy it is to become addicted to the drug.

Withdrawal refers to how painful it is to stop using the drug.

Tolerance refers to how much is needed over time to reach the same level of intoxication.

Reinforcement refers to the substance's ability to stimulate users to take it again, rather than use other drugs.

Intoxication refers to the level of mind alteration the drug induces.

WHICH DRUG IS RIGHT FOR YOU?

	DRUG PLUSES	DRUG MINUSES
Nicotine	Organic cigarettes available	None, except premature death
Heroin	May be smoked, sniffed, or injected, depending on mood	Sales finance the Taliban, religious fanatics who oppose the showing of Hollywood movies in the crucial Afghanistan market
Cocaine	Inspires delusions of grandeur	Inspires delusions of grandeur
Alcohol	A legal alternative to heroin	A legal alternative to Rophynol
Caffeine	One dose at Starbucks costs only $5.00	Must learn "barista" language to use this drug
Marijuana	Makes you mellow	Mellow stars don't last

LEGAL HIGH

There is always at least one "Dr. Feelgood" servicing Hollywood stars. These favored script (as in prescription) writers prescribe large quantities of pharmaceutical painkillers, such as Vicodin and OxyContin (aka "hillbilly heroin"), to stars who are suffering. Sometimes these physicians will open a file for you under an assumed name for privacy. Be careful. These doctors do not monitor your intake with your good health in mind. Don Simpson, the noted coproducer of *Flashdance* and *Bevery Hills Cop,* among other blockbusters, was found dead at his beautiful Bel Air estate with twenty-one different mind-altering drugs in his body, only one of which was illegal. The police found approximately twenty-two hundred pills scattered about his home. One of Simpson's psychiatrists was later disbarred for overprescribing drugs to him. No doctor was ever able to make him feel good again.

STAR QUESTION: What Should I Pack for Rehab?

The road to rehab is usually a rough one. But taking sanctuary in a seaside sanitarium can provide a nice break from the pressures of stardom. Aside from the obvious necessities—twenty-eight changes of clothes, organic body lotions, sheep-placenta-based-skin-firming pearls—any star visitor to an inpatient substance-abuse program is also advised to take the following items in order to stave off depression:

Organic chocolate
Positive reviews of recent films
Fan letters
Group portrait of household staff
Printout of most recent financial statement
Photographs of automobile collection

REHAB AMENITIES

Commonly used star rehabs, such as Promises Malibu and Passages Malibu, offer:

Gourmet chefs
Personal trainers
Exotic wood and marble finishes
Fireplaces
Juice bars
Library
Bedrooms with private marble baths
Massage
Acupuncture
Hypnotherapy
Gym

Arts and crafts room
Flat screen sixty-five-inch television
Eighty-seat auditorium for theatrical productions
View of the Pacific Ocean and mountains

STAR ISSUE: Celebrities Anonymous

The bylaws of Alcoholics Anonymous suggest that every meeting should be open to any person who believes they have a problem with alcohol. This means that anyone, from an odiferous street addict to a poorly dressed aggressive celebrity journalist (ACJ), can enter a meeting and possibly make a star uncomfortable. To avoid disturbing or troublesome contact with less-desirable fellow alcoholics and addicts, some stars have skirted the AA rule and have established private meetings. Every day of the week in New York and Los Angeles, celebrity lushes on the wagon, and their specially invited friends, gather for unofficial AA meetings in private homes. Your agent or publicist can secure an invitation, which is necessary to attend these pseudo-AA meetings.

STAR KNOWLEDGE: Upbeat Answers to Press Questions Regarding Your Rehab

The following statements have been effectively used by fellow stars and their publicists. You may quote or modify them to suit your current situation.

Star Statements

- "I have chosen to seek out professional assistance and am committed to traveling a healthier road with the support of my family, friends, and fans."
- "After realizing that I had a disease that was taking control of my life, I decided that the best way for me to regain my health was to enter a treatment facility."
- "I'm grateful for the love and support I've gotten from my wife, my entire family, my business associates, and my friends."

- "I got caught up in my new lifestyle and got carried away with drugs and alcohol. Once I realized this, I voluntarily checked myself into a detox facility for my own health and well-being."

Publicist Statements

- "[Your name here] was uncomfortable with the way that he was living his life and found the courage to deal with his disease."

- "[Your name here] is a self-aware and smart man who has decided that a fuller life awaits him without alcohol."

- "Due to a stressful year, [your name here] made the decision to enter a program at [name of rehab here]."

- "Following the advice of his doctors, [your name here] has entered an undisclosed rehabilitation hospital."

- "[Your name here] has every intention of completing his treatment so he can continue his dream of entertaining people and making them laugh. He appreciates everyone's concerns and thanks them for respecting his privacy."

INNER-CHILD CARE

Many recovering people report feelings of living under a "pink cloud" in the first few weeks after giving up their substance abuse. But reality invariably sets in, and the urge to use returns. When this happens to a star, his manager will often hire a personal babysitter to monitor the star's activity twenty-four hours a day, seven days a week, to prevent him from giving in to his urges. The cost: up to $500 an hour for a physician, less for a social worker.

CELEBRITY WORSHIP

It can be difficult to understand God when you are often worshipped like one. But even successful stars and IPs reach a point in their careers when the dark night of the Hollywood soul crashes down. Fortunately, two spiritual options are available right next door to each other on Sunset Boulevard. Both were founded by celebrities.

CHOOSING YOUR RELIGION

Los Angeles is the world's center of spirituality. On any given night, you can attend a dervish dance workshop, a fundamentalist Christian political fund-raiser, or a Native American sweat lodge ceremony sponsored by a group of one-legged lesbian Wiccans. With such a variety of spiritual programs available, it's important for a star to focus only on those religions that fit well with his or her lifestyle and career. The following chart will help you choose among the most hospitable religions/spiritual practices.

	Higher Power	Location of God	Belief System	Special Beliefs	Life After Death?	Cost of Faith
Catholicism	God	Heaven	A lovely virgin gave birth to God's only son while lying on a donkey's bed	Even though Jesus was a Jew, he didn't get into Kabbalah	If you work at it	Guilt
Scientology	You find God inside yourself after undergoing expensive "auditing" sessions	Los Angeles	The power of your spirit is limitless; psychiatry is for sissies	An alien despot named Xenu destroyed men's spirits eons ago	Scientology can help resuscitate your career	Can cost hundreds of thousands of dollars
Ramtha's School of Enlightenment	35,000-year-old spirit named Ramtha from the long-gone continent of Lemuria, which was located near Atlantis	A busty, Germanic blonde named JZ Knight channels Ramtha's thoughts	C + Energy = R (consciousness plus energy equals reality)	You can heal yourself with the Blue Body from the fourth plane of existence	Many lives left to live	Seminars at JZ's Washington state ranch start at $1,000
Kabbalah	Madonna	Los Angeles	Kabbalah is "the original technology of life"	Purchasing red bracelets and special water brings you closer to God	Yes, and you might get to hang out with angels while you're there	Kabbalah keychain: $10.00; Power of Kabbalah study kit: $495
Godcasting	Technology	Your iPod	Download sermons and listen to them on the freeway	Cleverness is next to godliness	As long as you have a valid AppleCare service agreement	Downloads are free; iPods cost up to $500

Self-Realization Fellowship Temple and Ashram Center

Founded in 1937 by Paramahansa Yogananda, the bestselling author of *Autobiography of a Yogi,* this temple encourages the faithful to use meditation and study to get to know God. Stars connect well with the idea that "He is your Self."

Church of Scientology

Founded in 1954 by bestselling science-fiction writer and global adventurer L. Ron Hubbard, the church headquarters are in a large blue building on L. Ron Hubbard Way, a stone's throw from the Self-Realization Fellowship Temple. Scientology has many star adherents, who follow the church's aims of creating a world without insanity, criminals, or war, where people can prosper and fulfill their potential as immortal spirits called *thetans.*

HOLLYWOOD SECRET: Using Religion to Your Advantage

While religions have always been quite profitable on the institutional level, in recent years various stars have banked fantastic box office on their own by marketing their faith. Here are Ten Commandments of Selling Your Religion:

- Pick a controversial religion and make a movie about it.
- If you already have a religion and it is not controversial, pick a little-known, much-disputed or archaic aspect of that religion to identify with (i.e., if you are a Muslim, go with Sufism; if you are Jewish, follow the rebbe; if you are a Christian, pick something creative from the Book of Revelations).
- Whether it is true or not, claim that you are financing the movie with your own cash, which will further your reputation as a fanatic.
- Have the deepest faith allowable by law.
- Don't be afraid of alienating "people of other faiths." The resulting publicity will be to your benefit.
- Choose a violent or perversely sexual subtext for the movie.

- Keep dialogue to a minimum to ease the translation into crucial foreign markets.
- Hire a discreet marketing company to secretly foment a grassroots promotional campaign among churches, temples, mosques, or whatever religious avenues are available to you.
- Respond to all press criticism with veiled threats from God.
- Pray all the way to the bank.

CHAPTER 4

MILKING IT
SELF-EXPLOITATION FOR FUN AND PROFIT

HONORING YOUR INNER PUBLICIST

It may appear that your fellow Hollywood stars effortlessly generate publicity with every smile, wardrobe malfunction, or half-baked utterance. But in truth, good PR takes thought, perseverance, action, and a team of professionals backing you up. You can keep your name in the news with a variety of tactics, from shamelessly denying that you desire fame to clambering for it. Or by doing both at the same time. Get married or get divorced. Jump rope for charity or jump bail. Have a child and devote yourself to his care, or leave your pregnant wife for another star. It doesn't really matter what you do, as long as you get the word out in advance. Your publicist will let you know when you've gone over the line. The moment a publicist says, "We've done enough publicity for this movie," you'll know the true meaning is, "You've become an embarrassment to yourself, this production, and my reputation. It's time to keep your mouth shut."

SELF-EXPLOITATION

You don't have to be a great, or even a good, actor to be a box office draw. You just have to generate buzz. That mainly comes from getting yourself in the magazines and newspapers, on TV, and on the Web. There are several approaches to doing this.

- *"I hate the whole publicity thing."*
  Someone taking this approach might agree to be interviewed by a prominent publication or TV show, only to spend the entire interview saying things like, "I don't want the press and don't need the press. Why would anyone want to know about me?" This anti-interview interview technique challenges the media's hegemony and is a surefire way to get quoted in every media outlet on the globe. It's a perennial strategy that somehow remains fresh, no matter how many stars use it.

- *"I am special, and I'd like to share that with the world."*
  A risky position to take, because even fans sometimes know that you're not. But when all else fails, a good display of brash ego almost always gets your name out there.

- *"I'd like the world to know about my new love."*
  Whether it is a new car or yacht, a starlet, or your daughter's lesbian lacrosse coach, your new fixation will fascinate the masses.

- *"I love my fans, and I do it all for them."*
  Pandering has worked for business professionals for thousands of years, but in Hollywood this approach usually only leads to midrange publicity. Often used by stars accused of pedophilia or murder.

- *"I am an artiste."*
  A surefire path to failure, except in those few boho urban neighborhoods that still have art-film houses. On the other hand, this is almost guaranteed to make you popular in France.

- *"My first love has always been music, and God has blessed me with the talent to rap with a Minnesota accent, so I'm going to fulfill His wishes. The acting thing is just a way to support that."*
  Unfortunately, you can fit the number of star actors who've become star musicians on top of a little piece of crack cocaine. This approach will get you profiles in *People*, *Rolling Stone*, and *Blender*, but you'll be portrayed as a deluded

poseur. As you tour the small bars and halls of America, "this acting thing" will soon fall by the wayside, and you'll find yourself sleeping in the van.

- *"I'm recovering from [fill in the blank: Sex. Drugs. Booze. Chocolate. Bulimia. Hepatitis C]."*
Your first recovery announcement will draw sympathy. Your second will draw mixed publicity. But by the third or fourth time in recovery, you'll begin to appear desperate, and your PR power will be vastly reduced. Proceed with caution.

HOLLYWOOD SECRET: Walk of Fame Demystified

To apply for a terrazzo and brass star with your name inset on the Hollywood Walk of Fame, download the application form from the Hollywood Chamber of Commerce (www.hollywoodchamber.net). Mail it with a self-addressed stamped envelope to The Hollywood Chamber of Commerce, 7018 Hollywood Boulevard, Hollywood, California 90028. Approximately twenty out of the two hundred nominations received each year are selected.

The fine print, from the Chamber of Commerce, says:

> It is understood that the cost of installing a star in the Walk of Fame, upon approval, is $15,000 and the sponsor accepts the responsibility for arranging for payment to the Hollywood Historic Trust, a 501-3 charitable foundation.

STAR KNOWLEDGE: The Publicist

Publicists are curious and powerful creatures who must be fed, stroked, and trained. In return, they will protect you from shame, increase your visibility when it suits you, and boost your career in immeasurable ways. Two large companies now control the outflow of star access, forming a sort of Hoover Dam across the river of celebrity confession. These firms—Baker/Winokur/Ryder and Interpublic (which owns the PR powerhouses of PMK/HBH, Rogers & Cowan, and Bragman Nyman

Cafarelli)—represent so many desirable stars that they can threaten to withhold access in the future if a journalist produces a negative story. This is good for you. Stars use clout-free independent publicists at their peril.

THE TRUTH

In the last decade, literary, art, and film scholars have begun to blur the boundaries between fiction and nonfiction. Naturally, PR agents have followed suit by asking stars to pretend that their lives are very similar to the character they played in their latest film. During the promotion period of your new release, you'll be asked to tell fictional nonfictions to reporters. Let's say your latest character is a one-legged mountain climber:

Journalist: *What prepared you for this role?*

You: *Well, as a child, I often climbed glacial peaks with a wise, one-legged Sherpa as my guide.*

Journalist: *That's amazing.*

You: *Yes, it is.*

Journalist: *That must have really helped you when you were climbing one-legged up the mountain in the movie, searching for your lost friend.*

You: *Yes, I felt very close to that character. I have great empathy for one-legged mountain climbers. It's a very difficult thing to do.*

According to the tired standards of the past, this information isn't true. You never climbed a mountain as a kid, and a stunt double did the actual hobbling uphill in the movie. (The insurance company would never allow you to risk your neck.) But according to the more fluid definitions of modern scholars, it's enough that you believe, or even pretend to believe you did this. And if your audience sees you all sunburned and windswept on a talk show, they'll think, "Wow," not "Wow, that's good makeup and hair!" They'll buy more tickets. And there's no disputing the reality of the bottom line.

HOW GOSSIP GETS INTO CIRCULATION

By RP standards, celebrity gossip is big business.

- Top gossip columnists and celebrity TV reporters can earn several hundred thousand dollars a year.
- These top gossipers (TGs) depend on a network of lower-level spies—down-on-their-luck journalists, bartenders, club owners, low-level celebrities, and others—to phone in tips, such as celebrity sightings, for which they might receive $300.
- In addition, nightclubs and restaurants will pay these bottom-feeding gossipers as much as $1,000 a month to place in the gossip columns items mentioning their business.
- Then there are the publicists hired by the stars themselves who have a symbiotic relationship with the TGs. Most commonly, these publicists will call the TGs directly when they have good gossip about their client. The publicity is worth a fortune for both sides. But publicists will also curry favor by passing on gossip items about people they don't even represent. They'll give a TG a bunch of tidbits for free and bank a favor as payment. Then, when one of their own star clients gets into a messy situation, they'll draw on their chits by asking the TG not to report it.

The Hollywood gossip industry operates like a mini commodities market, only the haggling is over celebrity dirt rather than pork jowls. All these people want to make a living off your personal life. Given the brutish nature of professional gossipers, all of whom seem to thrive on revenge, it's best for a star not to wage war against a TG. Just try to live and let live. Fortunately, many top glossies are now owned by the same corporations that own the major Hollywood studios, allowing corporate functionaries to wage "awareness missions" that basically involve pressuring editors not to tarnish important star reputations.

THE GOSSIP UNIVERSE

TOP GOSSIPER

Star publicist

Corporate publicist

Publicist bent on revenge

Bottom-feeding gossiper

Rumor monger

DEVELOPING A SILVER TONGUE

At times you will be involved in a relationship of romantic convenience that's meant only to promote your latest project. If the media asks about the relationship, you may use the following adjectives to describe your "lover" (whom you may not know very well), according to your star personality. It is recommended, however, that you run this personality by your publicist or life coach beforehand:

STAR PERSONALITY	BOY DESCRIBING GIRL LOVER	GIRL DESCRIBING BOY LOVER
Private	Nice	Nice
Bubbly	Delightful	Wonderful
Cool in a '70s way	Really cool	Awesome
Serious	Very supportive	Totally caring
Untrustworthy	Great	Great
Endearing	My best friend	My best friend
Honest	Sincere	Funny
Sex addict	Gorgeous	Buff
Casual	A babe	A hunk
Intellectual	Super smart	Brilliant
Old-fashioned	Stunning	A man's man
Superficial	Hot	Totally, like, hot
Superficial but trying to change image	Very special	A very special someone
Humble	Gifted	Talented
Insecure	Incredibly gifted	Enormously talented

MONIKERS

Aggressive celebrity journalists (ACJs) like nothing more than to combine two celebrity names to make a clever moniker for the couple. For publicity purposes, when choosing a lover or spouse, it's best to find someone with a first or last name that will combine with your own to make a pleasing, mostly nonsensical sound. Avoid names that together sound harsh or form a word that you don't want to be associated with. For instance, imagine the disaster that could have befallen Faye Dunaway and Martin Sheen.

Recent Pleasing Name Combinations

Ben + Jennifer = Bennifer

Brad + Angelina = Brangelina

Tom + Kate = Tomkat

Potential Disasters

Val + Gina = Vagina

Doris + Rock = Dork

Justin + Cameron = JustInc

Petra + Rick = Prick

HOW TO TELL A JOKE

Even if you don't have a sense of humor, you must know how to tell a joke so you'll look good on television talk shows. You don't have to think up the joke—your agent or publicist will find a low-paid writer to do that—but you must deliver it well, even if you don't understand it. Here's what you need to know:

- Memorize and practice your joke a couple of times before you must deliver it, preferably when you are sober.
- Use appropriate material—no Catholic jokes when in Rome, for instance.
- Set the joke up with all the necessary details so you don't have to explain the punch line.
- Commit to your joke and don't waver while telling it.
- Speak slowly and with useful verbal emphasis.
- Keep it short.

- Use body language to bring home the punch line.
- If the joke fails, act as if it went over well. Laugh at yourself.
- Be humble and self-deprecating. The audience will know you are joking and will eat it up.

ANATOMY OF A TALK SHOW

Talk shows are elaborate ruses by which the hosts sell advertisements and you sell your image and upcoming movie. Here's how they work:

1. Your movie is set for release.
2. Your publicist calls their booker.
3. They tell your studio to pay for your travel expenses (which are considerable).
4. You tell them to pay.
5. In the end, you split it.
6. Your publicist and their producers work out what questions you will be asked.
7. You arrive at the green room at the last minute. You share this room with the other guests unless your publicist has forced the show to give you a private dressing room.
8. Your publicist makes sure they have your favorite drink in a mug to be placed next to you on set.
9. You watch the monologue or opening news on-screen in the dressing room.
10. You move to the stage, behind the curtain if there is a live audience.
11. The producer counts down.
12. The host introduces you.
13. You walk out and smile broadly, hug, or whatever is appropriate.
14. Three minutes of chitchat.
15. You praise your director, fellow actors, studio, family, and God.

16. Commercial break, during which the host says nothing to you.
17. Two more minutes of chitchat.
18. You exit during commercial break.
19. You return to your hotel room and wait for your mother to call and say that you were great but that she didn't really like what you were wearing.

"THIS IS AN OUTRAGE!": Pros and Cons of Expressing Anger

Anger is a powerful star tool. However, in public it must be handled properly so as not to draw cameras and upset fans. You must use all your performance skills when expressing anger in public so that you fall into the pro column, rather than the con column.

PRO	CON
You appear human.	*You appear psychotic.*
The public sympathizes.	*The public thinks you're a jerk.*
The offending paparazzi backs off.	*The photographers mass outside your door.*
You get sued (any publicity is good publicity).	*You get sued (star lawyers charge over $500 an hour).*

STAR ISSUE: To Be or Not to Be (Gay)

Even though there are gay politicians, lesbian rock stars, and prime-time TV shows highlighting the humorous lifestyles of clichéd homosexuals, it's generally believed that stars must stay in the closet or risk sinking their careers. Occasionally, an opportunistic "special friend" will spread rumors that he's had a homosexual relationship with a star, hoping to profit somehow from the allegations. There are three responses to this situation: Maintain an uncomfortable silence; hire someone to rough the person up (not recommended); file a lawsuit. The following excerpts from one lawsuit recently filed by a long-term, twice-married, very good-looking star show the value of responding in a tough, unflinching manner:

1. To promote his career as an actor in pornographic films, defendant _____ has concocted and spread the completely false story that he had a continuing homosexual affair with _____ and that this affair was discovered by Mr. _____'s wife, leading to their divorce. There is not a germ of truth in this vicious, self-promoting story. While _____ thoroughly respects others' rights to follow their own sexual preference, he is not a homosexual, had no relationship of any kind with _____, and does not even know him. . . .

2. Each and every part of the defendant's statement was unequivocally false. Mr. _____ is not and has never been a homosexual. . . .

3. _____'s defamatory statements are of the kind calculated to cause _____ harm in his profession and ability to earn. Because _____ is a motion-picture actor, he is dependent upon worldwide public acceptance of his films. Losing the respect and enthusiasm of a substantial segment of the movie going public (sic), would cost _____ very substantial sums. While plaintiff believes in the right of others to follow their own sexual preference, vast numbers of the public throughout the world do not share that view and, believing that he had a homosexual affair and did so during his marriage, they will be less inclined to patronize _____'s films, particularly since he tends to play parts calling for heterosexual romance and action adventure.

4. As a direct and proximate result of _____'s defamation, _____ has suffered and will suffer both personal and professional harm, including very substantial monetary damages in a sum not as yet known but which plaintiff is informed and believes and, on that ground, alleges will exceed the sum of $100 million.

5. _____'s publication of the defamatory story was fraudulent and malicious in that _____ concocted the entire story and issued it to the international media at a time when he knew _____ was going through a highly publicized marital separation. _____ did so for the purpose of publicizing himself at _____'s expense, knowing the story was completely false and that it would be repeated in the media throughout the world.

WHEREFORE, plaintiff prays judgment as follows:

1. For $100 million or such greater sum as shall be found

2. For punitive damages

3. For costs of suit and such other relief as the court deems proper

Soon after this lawsuit was filed, reports that this major star had hired the defendant to wrestle naked with him in a private wrestling ring disappeared from the world media.

MARRIAGE OF CONVENIENCE

To avoid being abandoned by their RP fan base in the ROW, many CGSs court straight or gay people of the opposite sex as a way of hiding their homosexuality. Called lavender marriages, these relationships are generally quite transparent, in that they are consummated several months before the star's latest movie is released and end soon after the publicity machine dies down. These also help to shield RP from having to ponder difficult thoughts about gender and sexuality.

TEN SUREFIRE ATTENTION-GETTERS

Clip and keep in your wallet for those occasions when you need a quick shot of publicity.

- Adopt a child, preferably one whose skin is a different color than your own
- Have a "secret" on-set affair
- Survive a tsunami, volcanic eruption, or other natural disaster
- Romance a major rock star
- Make your "last" picture before "quitting the business for good"
- Try to strangle a hotel desk clerk
- Get on an airplane drunk or stoned out of your mind

- Try to get married "privately" (just make sure photographers are hiding in the woods)
- Eat way too much, or way too little, and then talk about how you're going to get over it
- Try to beat your addiction to gambling, drugs, booze, or lap dancers

DOS AND DON'TS: Arrest

Negotiating the Walk

Keep your head up.
Do not attempt to hide.
Do not smile or frown. Remain neutral.
Walk tall.
Do not attempt to sign autographs while wearing handcuffs.

Mug Shot

Ask to shave first.
Do not look straight into the camera; profile left or right, to highlight your best angle.
Smile slightly.
Keep eyes bright.

Dealing with Fans on the Inside

Do not smile, wink, or blow air kisses.

STAR KNOWLEDGE: Hiring a Prison Coach

While star power may help you establish your innocence during the judicial process, it won't be much use if you are imprisoned. Many of your fellow inmates will have been incarcerated for years, if not decades, without access to feature films or *People, Us Weekly,* and *Star* magazines. They might not have a clue who you are. If you have the bad luck to be found guilty of an imprisonable offense, immediately hire a consultant to get you the shortest sentence allowable and to help you prepare for life on the inside.

Here's what to expect:

- New inmates stick out like a deer caught in someone's headlights.
- It may take several weeks for you to be registered to use the Inmate Telephone System. BlackBerries are not allowed. Your agent, if you still have one, will not be able to return calls.
- Script conferences will take place through glass partitions.
- Kosher and other religious dietary practices are generally honored, although vegetarian and vegan diets are difficult to follow inside the walls.
- While fellow inmates are often willing to play the role of personal trainer if asked, your workout will largely be done with resistance exercises (push-ups, sit-ups, pull-ups) and free weights. Elliptical trainers are virtually nonexistent inside.
- You'll have no trouble losing weight, if you choose, thanks to stress, poor diet, and your workout program.
- It will be nearly impossible to download music to your MP3 player, which you won't be allowed to use, anyway.
- Inmates may send flowers to their agent, producer, and fellow stars when the occasion arises.
- Most disputes are settled verbally; however, if you get into a physical altercation, the other inmates will disappear, leaving you to work it out on your own.
- Rape occurs, though it is rare. Most same-sex erotic needs are easily fulfilled with consensual partners.

FOOD FOR THOUGHT

Typically, political and social fund-raisers feed stars well and send them home with gift bags so that they feel good for helping the poor, diseased, or otherwise unfortunate people who are to benefit from the fund-raiser. But be warned: Some benefits hope to drive home a political point by not feeding you well. A recent Oxfam International benefit tried to educate stars about poverty by dividing them randomly into groups that reflected the daily food intake of people around the world. Fifteen percent of the celebrities were fed a high-income diet of stuffed chicken breast, vegetables, and potatoes; 25 percent were served rice and beans; and the remaining 60 percent sat on the floor for a meal of rice and water. Given the odds of being seated on the floor, it's wise for any star to have a snack before attending such a benefit. It's hard to sympathize with the poor when low blood sugar is making you cranky.

POLITICAL EXPLOITATION

Sometimes stars are so strongly identified with the characters they portray that even the most sophisticated citizens call on them for advice. For instance, during a debate in Washington over farm subsidies and the growth of corporate agriculture, Congress sought the "expert" testimony of three Hollywood stars. The women had recently played embittered, embattled, and noble farm wives in major theatrical releases. They gave "expert" testimony about the perils and hardships of farming life, even though none of them had recently worked in the fields. Politicians shame themselves with this type of fatuous grandstanding, and the stars who participate only look silly. Avoid testifying in character at all costs.

STAR QUESTION: May I Have an Ideology?

Yes, but you should keep it secret. Most stars have political viewpoints and so do their characters. But expressing them will cause you to lose fans, friends, and business opportunities, and your candidate most likely will not be elected. It's not uncommon for committed stars to claim that they will leave the country if the candidate they oppose is elected president. While this is a very effective short-term PR tool, it will backfire if your candidate actually loses and you face public pressure to sell your home and relocate to Paris, Johannesburg, or Port-au-Prince. You cannot maintain your status in a place that doesn't have valet parking for your hybrid. Scripts will never reach you. Your SP will diminish.

SETTING PARAMETERS (AND PERIMETERS)

Publicists will generally let a reporter know which subjects a star will discuss and which topics are off limits. Often, the off-limits subjects relate to a star's personal relationships. Since these relationships are what sell magazines these days, ACJs will often ask the questions, anyway. A star who is having a difficult day might then storm out of the interview, leading to even more headlines. To prevent such catastrophes, stars in the midst of newsworthy personal dramas need to resort to legal language. Recently, the lawyers for a major female star, whose on-set dalliance with a major male star had recently broken up his marriage to another major female star, asked journalists to sign the following agreement. The journalists were threatened with lawsuits and heavy fines if they broke the agreement.

> Interviewer will not ask Ms. _____ any questions regarding her personal relationships. In the event Interviewer does ask Ms. _____ any questions regarding her personal relationships, Ms. _____ will have the right to immediately terminate the interview and leave. The interview may only be used to promote the Picture. In no event may Interviewer be entitled to run all or any portion of the Interview in connection with any other story. . . . The interview will not be used in a manner that is disparaging, demeaning or derogatory to Ms. _____.

GOOD NEWS ABOUT JOURNALISTIC "INTEGRITY"

Journalists used to think of themselves as independent, muckraking outcasts. That is no longer the case. Most big-time journalists now earn

JOURNALISTIC INTEGRITY

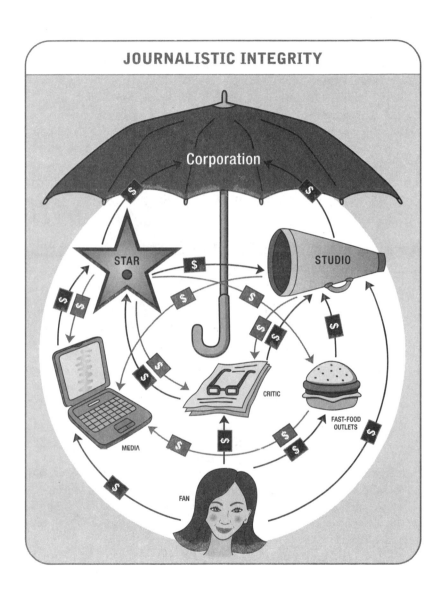

Corporation

STAR

STUDIO

CRITIC

MEDIA

FAST-FOOD
OUTLETS

FAN

corporate-size salaries and have all the attendant expenses—mortgage, private schools, leased gas guzzler, spa fees. Like every other upperclass person, they fear losing these perks. In order to preserve their position, they work desperately to please their bosses. These bosses, in the meantime, are trying to please the corporate board, who makes deals with other major corporations for advertising revenue—often the same corporations that own movie studios and distribution companies. To make matters even more complicated, many studios are financed by the same parent media conglomerate as the newspaper/magazine. So, to make a long story short, it's not easy for a journalist to say horrible things about a movie that is meant to enrich the corporation paying his salary.

STAR KNOWLEDGE: How to Air Kiss

Air kisses are widely used in Hollywood to confer intimacy where none actually exists and to prevent the transfer of dangerous germs. The air kiss is done between:

> *Members of the opposite sex*
> *Two straight women*
> *Two gay men*
> *A gay man and a straight man who is extremely*
> *comfortable with his masculinity*

It is extremely rare for two straight men to air kiss, unless they are old-school superpowers seeking to flaunt their self-assurance. An improperly executed air kiss can result in unpleasant physical contact, leading to injury or exchange of bodily fluids. A well-executed air kiss will take less than five seconds.

Step one. Approach your intended.

Step two. Place your hands lightly on, or about a half inch away from, your intended's shoulders; or, for two women only, hold her hands or wrists.

Step three. Lean forward toward your intended's left cheek, pursing your lips slightly.

Step four. Being careful not to make lip-to-cheek contact, make a slight smacking sound.

Step five. Retreat quickly and say, "How nice to see you again."

Optional flourishes:

A. The double air stroke. This is used on the red carpet at an awards show before cameras and crowds. After completing Step four, maintain your hands as in Step two and repeat Step three and Step four before winding up with Step five. But instead of saying, "How nice to see you again," say, "Oh, I didn't know you were up for an award. Good luck."

B. French Triple. The most ostentatious of air kisses, the French Triple is used in certain European circles and by stars who have threatened to flee the United States to escape persecution for their liberal political beliefs. Follow instructions in A above, with the addition of a third kiss. End kiss with these words: "Lots of love, baby."

STAR ISSUE: Handling the Paparazzi

Paparazzi is Italian for "buzzing insects." These celebrity photographers routinely follow stars into the dry cleaners, photograph their children at school, and chase them down the freeway. They invade the privacy of their beach houses with telephoto lenses and wait at the airport to photograph them leaving a fourteen-hour flight looking disheveled. Some of the biggest stars seem able to stroll through the camera-wielding hordes with ease, not letting the flashes get under their skin. Others, however, run from these photographers like frightened animals. The photographers, sensing fear, pursue even more relentlessly. In the last few years, this has led to fistfights and even to several car crashes—some fatal. Unfortunately, the paparazzi are part of your life now. How you handle them on any given day is a good gauge for how you are holding up to the extraordinary stresses of being rich, pampered, and adored. Here is a hypothetical situation, followed by typical star responses and their meanings:

Situation: You and a lovely specimen of the opposite sex leave lunch at the Ivy to face fourteen paparazzi on the sidewalk, cameras at the ready.

STAR RESPONSE	MEANING
Flip them the bird and curse their mothers	*Low self-esteem*
Pose for two minutes after which you ask them to respect your privacy	*High self-esteem*
Cry, moan, cover your head, fall to the ground, and writhe	*You are a good actor*
Jump into your Mercedes and slam on the gas. Weave down the freeway at ninety-five mph, the wild photographers on your tail	*Disregard for fellow man*
Let them do what they want; don't engage them in any way	*You are smart*
Lift your dress and show them you aren't wearing panties	*You have a new movie to promote*
Stick your tongue in your partner's mouth, even though one of you is gay and you both just ate garlic	*You have a new movie to promote*
Call the LAPD's threat management unit	*You want more publicity*

A PAPARAZZO SPEAKS

According to one London-based celebrity photographer, it's possible for stars and paparazzi to have a mutually beneficial relationship if it is based on respect and a recognition of one shared goal: profit. Jack Ludlam, of London Paparazzi (www.londonpaparazzi.com), admits that some photographers are "a pain in the ass." But he also says that many stars are just whiners. He suggests that stars and photographers work together to scratch one another's backs. "Why not just have a pleasant way of going about your work that doesn't involve drama and grief?" The secret, he says, is to accept that you will be photographed. Be polite and accommodating. Word will get around that you are a decent person. Then, when you ask for cooperation from the photographers on those occasions when you don't want to be shot, they'll respect you.

HOLLYWOOD SECRET: Racketeering

If you just can't bear being attacked by flashes every time you leave your house, consider filing a racketeering and conspiracy lawsuit against the paparazzi. Since photographers often chase celebrities in packs, federal antiracketeering laws might prevent paparazzi from taking your picture and selling it to magazines.

TEN REPORTERS' QUESTIONS YOU SHOULD ALWAYS ANSWER WITH A NO

Did you see the LA Times *review of your new movie?*

Do you find it difficult to get good roles at your age?

Is your marriage troubled?

Are you seeing _____ romantically?

Do you feel you had to "sell out" in order to become a star of your magnitude?

Are you gay?

Are you satisfied with your achievements?

Would you comment on the upcoming presidential contest?

Do you ever get tired of acting?

Are you the father?

FROM IDEA TO PRINTED PAGE

The Traditional Route

• Publicist lunches with magazine editor, hints at "access" to star who just happens to be opening a new movie in six months.

• Editor ponders which writer in her stable would pander enough to bag the story. Writer gets weak in the knees thinking of meeting actor.

• Editor begins to salivate at the thought of a cover with the star.

• Editor calls publicist. Publicist says maybe and suggests that a competing magazine is in the running.

• Editor freaks out. Begs writer to come up with an interview "scenario."

• Writer suggests one of the following: I hang out with star at the Grand Canyon for a week; I fly to Europe on star's jet, and we hang out; I spend the weekend skiing with star at Telluride.

• Star's publicist tells editor that writer will have one hour with star, with publicist and bodyguards present. Writer must submit questions in advance.

• Writer tells editor he can work with that level of "hanging out."

• "Interview" takes place at the Ivy, Chateau Marmont, or some other public place. Writer not allowed to ask questions. Publicist reads writer's questions and star responds. Writer tapes their conversation.

• Publicist chooses photographer for cover shot. A makeup artist ($5,000 a day), hairdresser ($5,000 a day), stylist ($15,000 a day), photographer ($80,000 a day), various assistants, caterers, and others gather to produce a beautiful shot.

• Writer produces a 5,000-word essay, using his or her "very intimate lunch" with the star as a hook.

• Editor has the art director enlarge all the pictures and cuts the text by 4,250 words.

• Cover shot means great newsstand sales for magazine and major publicity for the star.

New Paradigm Route

• Star breaks up with spouse and falls in love with another star; or, conversely, star falls in love with another star, denies it, and then breaks up with spouse (the latter scenario usually generates a full twelve months of publicity).

- Media outlets buzz and start demanding pictures and interviews for free.
- Star, by chance, has a new movie coming out. He or she maligns the "superficial, greedy, destructive media."
- Star contacts major photographer and proposes doing an elaborate "fictional" family scene, with the star and the love interest playing husband and wife, for a sixty-page spread in a major glossy magazine.
- Star and photographer retain rights to the "story."
- Magazine pays all photo shoot expenses and runs the story for free.
- Star and photographer resell the photos to magazines all over the world for $3–5 million.
- Star and new true love decide to get married.
- The couple sells the rights to their wedding photographs to a major glossy for $1.5 million.
- Couple retains the copyright and resells said photos all over the world.
- The income pays the $6-million cost of their wedding.
- Baby makes three. Reality show beckons.

WHEN TO LIE LOW

Very occasionally, no publicity is good publicity. It's best to keep totally quiet on the following occasions:

- When your movie is abysmal and headed straight to DVD. (On the other hand, if it is horrible and headed into the theaters, promote the heck out of it.)
- When your name and the words "sex" and "underage" are mentioned in tandem.
- Anything to do with politics.

◆◆◆

CHAPTER 5

THE GRIND

SIX DAYS A WEEK, SIX WEEKS IN A ROW, FOR ONLY $16 MILLION

WORK IS WHAT YOU LIVE FOR

In the early days, months, or possibly even years of a star's ascendance, hard work and long hours are necessary steps on the path to fame and doughlo. However, everything changes when you finally hit the big time. At a certain point, money becomes less of a lifestyle-enhancement tool—are two jets really more useful than one?—than a means for one-upmanship. The desire to be recognized as a great artist will grow as you sacrifice everything in your quest to be the very best minimal-dialogue action star, the sexiest leading lady, or the most sympathetic everyman on the screen. Universal acceptance becomes the goal as fame, power, and talent converge to propel you forward. The job will quickly start to feel like your life, a twenty-four-hours-a-day, seven-days-a-week struggle to keep your name in the public eye (except during stints in rehab, when the world stops spinning and stars are allowed time off). As such, maintaining your career requires much more than just acting your heart out in front of the cameras. It also requires acting off-camera, in the car, at home, and on vacation. A successful star's job is never done.

HOW TO BEHAVE

Teamwork and the credo "the show must go on" are the secrets to maintaining a successful star career. Even if the ROW sees you as a motorcycle-riding playboy with gangster DNA, to succeed over the long-term, you must be kind and hardworking on the job. The lead actor's tone and the director's tone together determine the mood of the set. You must treat even the lowest-level worker on the film with respect. And you must pull your weight. Every day there are dozens, if not hundreds, of people working together to make your movie great, at a cost of several hundred thousand dollars a day (not counting your salary). Each scene may require as many as two dozen takes, although five to ten is average. If you're lazy or distracted, you'll slow everyone down, and the end product won't be as good. Mediocre actors with great work ethics and decent personalities get more jobs than brilliant artistes with horrible reputations. This sense of teamwork and dedication is one of the more charming aspects of a star's life. So save your abusive comments for home. If you must be rude on the set, direct your remarks at personal assistants and barnacles.

MOVIE PRODUCTION TIMELINE

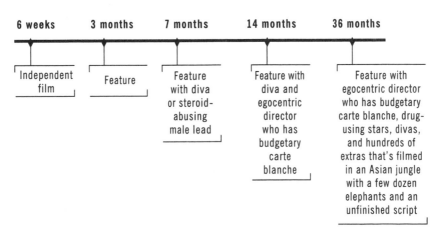

6 weeks	3 months	7 months	14 months	36 months
Independent film	Feature	Feature with diva or steroid-abusing male lead	Feature with diva and egocentric director who has budgetary carte blanche	Feature with egocentric director who has budgetary carte blanche, drug-using stars, divas, and hundreds of extras that's filmed in an Asian jungle with a few dozen elephants and an unfinished script

ON-SET HIERARCHY

1. Star
2. Producer and director (they vie for power)
3. Line/production manager (backs up the producer)
4. First assistant director
5. Director of photography
6. Important cast members
7. Wardrobe head
8. Makeup artists and hairdressers
9. Location manager
10. Unit manager
11. Secondary cast members
12. Crew
13. Star's good-looking "special friend"
14. Personal assistants

HOW TO ACT

"The secret of acting is sincerity. If you can fake that,
you've got it made."—GEORGE BURNS

"There is no me. I do not exist. There used to be a me,
but I had it surgically removed."—PETER SELLERS

You might have made it this far on your looks and charm. To remain in
the game, you must learn how to act—all the time. That means you must
learn to express the following emotions at will:

Admiration	*Compassion*	*Guilt*
Anger	*Desire*	*Happiness*
Anxiety	*Despair*	*Hope*
Boredom	*Disgust*	*Impatience*

Indignation	*Pity*	*Serenity*
Infatuation	*Pride*	*Shame*
Jealousy	*Rage*	*Shock*
Loneliness	*Regret*	*Sorrow*
Lust	*Relief*	*Sympathy*
Panic	*Sadness*	*Terror*

CHARACTER ACTING

If your agent is smart, at some point you'll be offered the ultimate role: yourself. The newest Hollywood genre, "Me Movies," has scripts that center around the real lives of the stars themselves. The prototypical Me Movie storyline involves a film star playing himself in a movie about himself. The star's mom and dad play themselves, as do the star's friends, acquaintances, and neighbors. An offshoot of reality TV, this type of movie can be a very easy acting job for any star.

STAR ISSUE: Danger

Despite all the explosions, crashes, beheadings, shootings, knifings, and fires in the typical movie, stars are never, ever put in danger. Professional stunt doubles are well paid to take risks, when necessary. And postproduction studios are used to insert the fires and other dangers the star is meant to encounter. The biggest risk a star faces in an action movie is not being able to act convincingly. It is a challenge for a star to look like he is walking through fire when none is present.

STUNTS

The Stuntwomen's Association of Motion Pictures and the Stuntmen's Association of Motion Pictures will refer stuntpeople—according to size, appearance, and skills needed—to perform the following stunts, among others, for safety-conscious stars:

Acrobatics

Aerial silk (parachuting)

Aerobics

Animal fighting

Archery

Bareback horse riding

Bike riding

Boat handling

Bodybuilding

Boxing

Bungee jumping

Camel riding

Car bailouts, crashes, jumps, and turnovers

Cheerleading

Cliff diving

Climbing

Contortionism

CPR

Dancing

Demolition derby driving

Drag racing

Driving cars and other vehicles

Escaping explosions

Falling down waterfalls

Fighting

Figure skating

Fire dancing and eating

Glass gags— breaking windows, jumping through windows

Golfing

Ground pounding

Gun shooting

Hand balancing

Hang gliding

Hatchet throwing

High-wire walking

Horse drags, falls, and throws

Ice hockey

Ice skating

Jet skiing

Juggling

Kayaking

Kiteboarding

Knife throwing

Martial arts

Miming

Motorcycle jumps and crashes

Piloting airplanes, balloons, and helicopters

Polo playing

Pratfalls

Racquetball playing

Rappelling

Rollerblading

Running

Singing

Skiing, snow boarding, and snowmobiling

Skydiving

Snorkeling

Stagecoach driving

Stair falling

Stilt walking

Street luging

Surfing

SWAT tactics

Sword fighting

Team roping

Trampoline jumping

Transferring from one horse, plane, or vehicle to another

Trapeze flying

Tumbling

White-water rafting

Wing walking

Wrestling

DOWNTIME

When the production has to switch from one scene to another, the technical work of moving equipment, changing sets, and other tasks can take several hours. This is your quality time, when you can retreat to your trailer (see pages 122–123) with your entourage of masseuses, bodyguards, trainers, coaches, spiritual advisers, and buddies to hang out and watch TV, read, or have the set doctor give you an injection of vitamin B_{12}. Some stars schedule a playdate with a special friend (a costar, cameraman, or professional brought in from the outside). On-set sex is both common and accepted, and star trailers generally have excellent suspension systems. Other stars meet with their Scientology teams for self-improvement sessions.

PERSONAL ASSISTANTS

When so much else in your world—fans, production costs, your waistline—feels out of your control, a personal assistant can offer much-needed relief. A good PA functions as an easily controlled commodity; when properly motivated through fear and gifts, abuse and promises, he or she will be as loyal as a good dog. Be sure to tempt your PA with the chance to meet other stars, which tends to excite RP. PAs are easy to hire, and easy to fire, as there is always another attractive young person waiting in the wings to replace the one you are dumping. Here is a template for a help-wanted ad you can use when searching for your next PA:

Star seeks well-organized technogeek for personal assistant. Must be charismatic, intelligent, and capable. Hunky or perky a plus. Must drive, type, take dictation, and be able to cook, clean, and pet-sit. Hair and makeup experience a plus. Must be polite, know proper etiquette, and be able to plan parties, make travel arrangements, and buy gifts. Fashion and interior design skills a plus. Single people only, please, as PA must be on call 26 hours a day, 8 days a week.

TEN TASKS FELLOW STARS HAVE DELEGATED TO THEIR PERSONAL ASSISTANTS

- Buy last-minute gifts for "special friends"
- Find out just what the pool boy has in mind
- Secure passports, licenses, and other documents
- Take stool samples to doctor
- Pick up dates and escorts
- Harvest cash from the ATM
- Compose romantic e-mails and send them to your lovers
- Lose arguments with you in public so that you appear to be a winner
- Take dictation while you're on the toilet
- Hire maid, and fire her when she screws up

STAR KNOWLEDGE: Anatomy of a Screenplay

Hollywood movies are not known for originality, and you should avoid those that have risky stories. Billion-dollar-grossing films are generally based on comic-book-type stories and feature young heroes who have sexless relationships. Dialogue is limited in order to make the film work better in non-English overseas markets. Occasionally a quirky or deep story will find its way through the studio system, but generally star movies follow strict formulas. The screenplay, which may be rewritten over time by as many as a dozen writers and could cost up to $5 million, has three main elements: the plot, the characters, and the premise. It's not difficult to graft the characters from one film onto the plot and premise of another (i.e., put the Terminator character in the role of Spider-Man) or to join the plot of one movie to the characters and premise of another (marry the plot of *The Wizard of Oz* with the characters and premise of *Working Girls*). The three-act blockbuster structure of introduction, dramatic situation, and resolution is mirrored in every star's life: A star is born, a star lives, a star dies.

TECHNICAL ASPECTS OF THE SCRIPT

- Almost all scripts are written so that one page equals one minute of screen time. Therefore, most scripts are 90–120 pages long. In a 90-page script, the characters are introduced in the first 15 pages.
- From pages 15–30, something happens to change the main character's (the protagonist's) life. This character faces a major moral question (i.e., Should I blow up Moscow to save my old buddy?).
- About page 30, the protagonist faces a setback (Oh, no, I don't have enough frequent-flier miles to get to Russia).
- Pages 30–90 reveal a series of forward and backward movements, frequently with flashbacks and backstory, which are meant to support the story and entertain the audience.
- At about page 60, the protagonist has a realization of sorts (Wow, all these years I should have used a credit card that gives me mileage points; I think I'm going to take better care of myself in the future; and, meanwhile, I'm going to save money for that ticket).
- On page 80, the protagonist faces yet another crisis (Those pesky Russki customs agents want to confiscate my nukes).
- Then on page 85, the movie reaches its climax (the protagonist has wired his explosives under the Kremlin and pushes the button).
- This crowd-pleasing sequence is followed by the resolution (I saved my friend; I will forever be a reluctant hero—through at least three sequels).

THE POPCORN FACTOR

It's a reality every star must face: You are no more than a glorified candy salesperson, and your scripts reflect this sad truth. Movie theaters have to give up to 80 percent of ticket sales to the studio. Since theaters keep all concession-stand profits for themselves, candy, popcorn, hot dogs, and soda are big business, making the seat cup holder an important movie-industry innovation. In effect, movies are used to glean massive profits from food: At some cinemas, a small soda yields a 91 percent profit, and a small popcorn earns a whopping 96 percent return. The more people who pass through the concession stand each night, the bigger the profits. If a movie runs longer than 128 minutes, it can only be shown twice in an evening, rather than three times, thus reducing popcorn income by one-third. Therefore, cinemas don't like booking long movies, and studios don't like making them. Which means most movies run just under two hours, no matter what the story is.

FILM FESTIVALS

There are hundreds of film festivals around the world each year. Other than Cannes, most will have no effect at all on your career. However, a few offer great fun or a great vacation in an exotic locale (all expenses paid, of course). Try these:

Cannes: *La grand-mère des festivals de film,* Cannes is where starlets doff their tops for the cameras, moguls flood discos with bottles of champagne, and stars loll about on yachts, waiting to make an appearance. Anything goes, and a lot of deals are finalized here. Local delicacies include fresh garden snails in the shell.

Caribbean International Film Festival: The primary attraction of this film festival is the beach, since it rotates among Caribbean islands like St. John. It offers a great reason to escape in late November, just as gray, slightly chilly skies descend on Hollywood. And it's tax deductible. Local delicacies include seaweed beverages.

Sundance: Park City, Utah, in January means funny fur hats, huge SUVs, and schussing down the slopes of this first-rate ski resort. Lots of deal-making going on. And the swag is the best of any festival. Swag bags can be worth $20,000. Corporations also set up "Star Rooms" that are basically luxury convenience stores filled with valuable free gifts for invited stars. Local delicacies include green-bean-and-mushroom-soup casserole.

Kerala International Film Festival: Located in Thiruvananthapuram, India, this festival is worth a visit just so you can amaze fellow stars with your ability to pronounce the name of the city, which honors the fabled serpent god Anantha. Local delicacies include rice dough string hoppers.

Hamptons International Film Festival: Held in Easthampton, New York, and the surrounding area, this festival packs in an inordinate number of stars who are drawn by the broad white sand beaches, exclusive restaurants, and proximity to other power stars, directors, and IPs. With weekly beach house rentals topping $20,000, be sure the studio foots the bill. Local delicacies include clam pie.

NEGOTIATING THE CANNES FILM FESTIVAL

Cannes is a relatively small city in Southern France with sunny weather. That, rather than any link to the cinema, is why it's home to the most influential film festival in the world. In the early 1930s, as fascism gained currency, the first big international film festival took place in Venice, Italy. It soon became obvious that most of the winning films were from fascist-leaning countries like Germany and Italy. In 1939, Jean Renoir's *La Grand Illusion* was widely believed to be the best film in the festival, but the prize was shared by two lesser entries, a German film produced by Joseph Goebbels's Ministry of Propaganda, and an Italian movie made by Mussolini's son. The French, American, and British representatives at the festival were outraged and quickly resigned. They chose to start a festival in Cannes. In 1954, the coveted Palme d'Or prize was introduced, the sculpture based on a sketch done by the director Jean Cocteau. That same year, the French actress Simone Sylva revealed her breasts on the beach, starting a long tradition of well-endowed starlets exposing themselves for the cameras. (As a star, you do not need to expose yourself for publicity, no matter what anyone tells you. Leave that to the up-and-comers.) Brigitte Bardot made quite an impression this way, several years, if not decades, running. Today Cannes is the most important and well-publicized festival in the world, with nearly a hundred films from

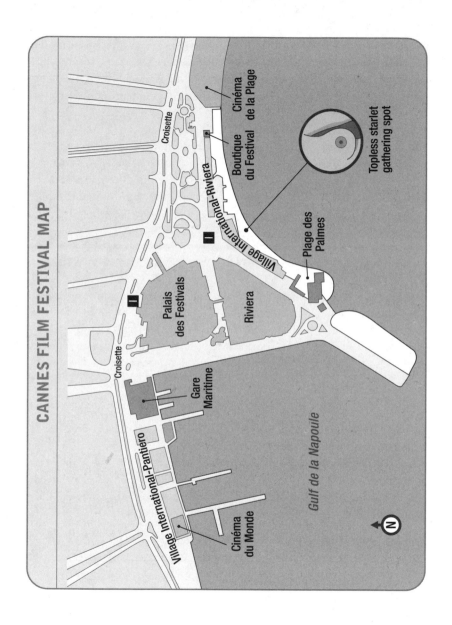

CANNES FILM FESTIVAL MAP

Cinéma
de la Plage

Cinéma
de la Plage

Boutique
du Festival

Topless starlet
gathering spot

Croisette

Village International-Riviera

Plage des
Palmes

Palais
des Festivals

Riviera

Croisette

Gare
Maritime

Village International-Pantiéro

Cinéma
du Monde

Gulf de la Napoule

N

around the globe competing for prizes. Each year over two hundred thousand people attend the festival, including about one thousand writers and directors, four thousand distributors, five thousand producers, four thousand journalists, and a dozen or so true stars.

STAR QUESTION: What Should I Pack for Cannes?

Umbrella (it often rains)
Linen and other light fabrics (temperatures reach the mid eighties)
Sandals (although flip-flops are discouraged)
Tuxedo (all evening events are black tie)
Ball gown
Sensible heels (red carpets can be treacherous)
Swimsuit (nothing modest, or you will be made fun of in the press)
Inhaler (everyone smokes and your allergies will kick up)

STAR POWER: Exploiting Your Own Charisma

Natural charisma is the secret to SP. And it can be enhanced, according to Karl Hans Welz, inventor of the Chi Generator and other "life force boosting radionics devices that are meant to have an energetic steroid effect on the user's personality." Welz claims the Chi Generator uses "orgonite" to "accumulate orgone energy and emit it within a twenty-foot radius through scalar wave disturbance." Amazingly, the machine is purported to work even when it is turned off (passive mode). But plug it in (active mode), says Welz, and the black box "ramps up life force energy projection." There's even a "Transfer Disk TD 99" that you can put in your pocket to receive the ramped-up energy from your Chi Generator even if you're thousands of miles away! The Chi Generator costs just $129.00.

ROMANIA: The New Burbank

This mountainous, little-developed country on the Baltic Sea is the legendary home of Count Dracula, but until recently it had few other Hollywood connections. However, these days more and more producers are drawn by the low costs associated with filming in Romania. Film technicians there are paid yearly salaries roughly equal to your monthly hair bill, and extras earn barely enough for just one feast at the Ivy. Directors like the unspoiled landscapes. Unfortunately, stars often find the country unusual and slightly inhospitable. To help prepare you for your visit, here is a typical day's menu in Romania:

Breakfast
Mămăligă (corn meal mush) with eggs
Lapte batut ("turned over" milk, slightly sour)

Lunch
Ciorba de burts (tripe soup)
Pirjoala Moldoveneasca (Moldavian hamburger)
Must (slightly fermented grape juice)

Dinner
Saramura de Crap (grilled carp with pepper)
Calugaresc (vegetables stewed in oil)
Papansh (donuts with cream)
Tzuica (plum brandy)
Nescafé

THE STUDIO JET

Use of a studio private jet is the most important status symbol in Hollywood, and it's a standard part of contract negotiations. If your lawyer and agent can't negotiate this perk, get new representation. One aircraft-obsessed star who pilots his own crafts says jets help his art by allowing him to travel the world and meet lots of people who inspire his characters, but for most stars, a jet is just a really comfortable perk. Jets wait for you, so there's never a mad dash to the airport, and your limo pulls right up to the plane, out of reach of paparazzi. The food is great, there's plenty of room for carry-ons, and customs officials usually come right onto the plane to process your paperwork. Sometimes a second jet is needed to transport a star's hair and makeup people or even personal effects (a studio once spent $60,000 to bring a star's luggage back from Europe via jet). Jets have been dispatched across the country to pick up Nathan's hot dogs and special-recipe chili. Most studios use Gulfstream IV jets, which seat about twelve people comfortably and cost about $25 million. Many stars have to go through an intermediary at the studio to get use of the jet, and at times it won't be available. But the biggest stars usually lease jet time with a company like NetJets and bill the studio $3.65 million for one hundred hours' use of a G-IV plus tens of thousands of dollars a month in maintenance fees and $3,200 an hour for travel time. It is also possible to hire jets using the Marquis Jet Black Card, which is a prepaid debit card ($250,000 is a standard amount). Have the bill sent to your studio, of course.

STAR KNOWLEDGE: The Kiss

It's hard enough to speak lovingly on camera to someone you may despise. But on-screen kissing requires even greater acting skills. Here's an effective step-by-step approach:

Step 1. Ask your makeup artist to examine your partner's mouth for any oral herpes sores.

Step 2. Insist that your fellow star brush his or her teeth and use mouthwash.

Step 3. Hug. A lingering embrace can help you prepare for the deed to come.

Step 4. Go in for the kiss but aim your lips so they hit your partner's lower lip, to form a double-decker sandwich that prevents any possibility of French-kissing.

Step 5. Inhale deeply through your nose to relax and let your lips slide across your partner's lips.

Step 6. Pretend your partner is someone you would really love to kiss.

Step 7. Act like you mean it.

Step 8. Don't wipe your mouth until the director says "cut."

STAR ISSUE: EXPOSURE

Nude scenes can be fun, if you look great and are comfortable with your body. If you aren't, they're an ordeal. It's important for every star to include provisions in the contract that outline just how much skin he or she will reveal. Here are some excerpts from a rider used not long ago by a star:

♦♦♦

NUDITY RIDER

(1a) Artist's nude scenes and simulated sex scenes shall be in accordance with the screenplay . . . and any changes which increase . . . the Artist's nude and/or simulated sex scenes shall be subject to Artist's absolute approval.

(1b) Artist shall have the absolute right to change Artist's mind and not perform in any nude or simulated sex scene . . .

(1c) No pubic hair may be shown nor any of Artist's lower frontal/genital or lower posterior nudity. Artist's breasts and nipples shall not be shown unless Artist, in consultation with the director, agrees to show Artist's nipples and/or breasts. In the filming of nude and/or simulated sex scenes, Artist shall not be required to actually be nude (Artist may wear a bodysuit, pasties, underwear, or other appropriate undergarments as long as such clothing does not materially interfere with the photography of the scenes). . . .

(2b) Artist shall not be required to simulate the performance of the following sex acts: sex acts with another woman other than kissing and touching (but not touching breasts, the pubic area, or buttocks). . . .

(5) The dailies of any nude or simulated sex scene may be viewed only by Artist, the director, and such members of the key crew whom the producer designates in good faith as having essential business reasons for viewing such dailies. . . .

(6) No still photographers . . . shall be present on the set during the filming of any nude or simulated sex scene. . . .

CREDITS

When the credits roll, your name should dominate the screen. Otherwise, fellow stars may laugh at you behind your back. Demand that

- in the movie and all promotional material your name be the same size as the movie title
- no other person or entity receive larger credit
- your name appear before other stars' names
- your likeness be as large or larger than any other star's

STAR PERKS

Sure, a star needs to be a team player, pitching in when needed and working just as hard as everyone else. But stars also need perks, which are a key indicator of SP. There are usually thirty to forty perk points in each movie contract. One star insists that the studio build him a regulation-size basketball court at each location. Another asks for water that has been blessed by a shaman. Another asks for three on-set trailers: one for himself, one for his gym equipment, and one for his entourage. Although perks can add $5 million to a movie's costs, stars generally get what they ask for. Here's the list of perks one star got in recent negotiations:

- A jet for any necessary air travel, if possible. If not, then seven first-class round-trip tickets for star, family, employees, and friends
- Private home or two-bedroom "presidential suite," plus $3,500 per week nonaccountable per diem
- Luxury automobile with driver plus luxury convertible for those occasions when star wants to drive

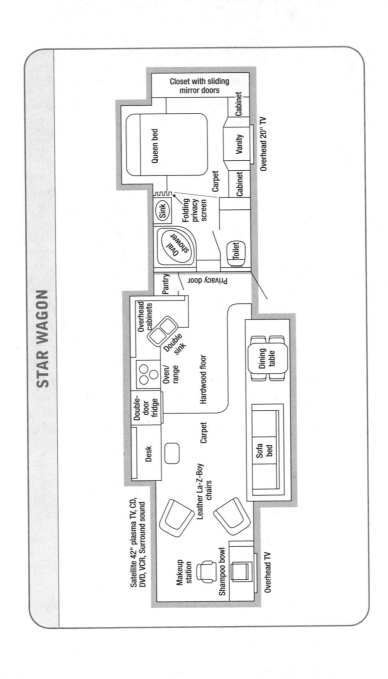

STAR WAGON

Closet with sliding mirror doors

Queen bed

Cabinet

Vanity

Overhead 20" TV

Carpet

Cabinet

Sink

Folding privacy screen

Oval shower

Toilet

Pantry

Privacy door

Overhead cabinets

Double sink

Oven/ range

Hardwood floor

Double-door fridge

Desk

Carpet

Satellite 42" plasma TV, CD, DVD, VCR, Surround sound

Leather La-Z-Boy chairs

Makeup station

Shampoo bowl

Sofa bed

Dining table

Overhead TV

- Rental cars for hairstylist, dresser, and makeup artists (who earn $5–7,000 a day)
- Subsidy of up to $12,000 to pay for personal publicist during filming
- The right to approve all substantial changes to the screenplay
- Right to approve star's physician, makeup artists, hairdressers, dialogue coaches, stand-ins, stunt doubles, and brand-name products star holds as part of product-placement guarantees
- Invitations to all premieres for star and six guests (fifteen for main premiere), including first-class round-trip airfare for star and coach fare for three guests, plus luxury hotel rooms; invitations, hotel rooms, and coach fare to main premiere for star's bodyguard, makeup artist, publicist, and assistant
- Two cellular phones
- Maximum fourteen-hour workdays; maximum five-day workweek
- No pickup at hotel or house before 7:00 A.M.
- Right to approve caterer or subsidy for personal chef
- Right to keep all clothes and jewelry used in filming, excluding rentals
- Pilates machine for personal use
- No cigar or cigarette smoking on set
- Armed bodyguards at all times

HOLLYWOOD SECRET:
The Star Wagon Supreme

This trailer, a forty-three-foot fifth wheel that is pulled behind a truck, has three slide-out sections that allow for a variety of rooms. There is an entertainment center with a sound system and a satellite-driven forty-two-inch plasma-screen TV with DVD/VCR; a living room with leather La-Z-Boy swivel recliners and a sleeper sofa; a bedroom equipped with a queen-size bed, shower, and twenty-inch TV; and a kitchen with a side-by-side refrigerator, stove, and microwave. The dining area seats four. At the rear is the star's makeup station and shampoo bowl. Hardwood floors, carpet, wood paneling, and luxurious drapes make this trailer star-worthy.

CHAPTER 6

MONEY GETTING
WHAT YOU DESERVE

MONEY IS THE HOLLYWOOD ART

Marilyn Monroe once said, "Hollywood is a place where they'll pay you a thousand dollars for a kiss and fifty cents for your soul." More than ever, studios are in the business of making money, rather than movies, in a grand scheme that cross-links corporate subsidiaries in a network of product tie-ins, foreign markets, DVD sales, spin-offs, product placement, and, almost vicariously, the movies themselves. Stars are central to this business and are therefore remunerated very well. But the money does not come easily. Teams of agents and lawyers negotiate endlessly for the star—the contract negotiations for one heavily accented action star's movie contract spanned eighteen months. Because they are perceived as being so important to a film's success, most stars end up doing very well. They receive money from acting, troll dolls made in their likeness, and nonmovie investments. Florence Lawrence, who in the early twentieth century became the first celebrity actor, even profited on the side from inventing the automotive turn signal and a primitive brake light. Given their important artistic contributions to the culture, stars deserve to get paid. Although that doesn't mean they need to brag about how much they get. When asked how it feels to have earned $450 million in the last few years, with $100 million more expected from an upcoming movie, the well-balanced star will insist that he's not in the business for money or fame; it's the art, the chance to connect with an audience of millions, that gets him out of bed in the morning. Thank God.

STUDIO REVENUES

Six international corporations run Hollywood:

Time Warner
Viacom
Fox
Sony
NBC Universal
Disney

These corporations have enormous influence over world culture, not to mention your career. Together, the six corporations earn the following sums from selling stars' images:

VIDEO/DVD	FREE TV	MOVIE THEATERS	PAY TV
$18.9 billion	*$11.4 billion*	*$7.48 billion*	*$3.36 billion*

Total: $41.14 billion

BLURRY IMAGE

Unfortunately, the film industry is famous for blurring more than its accounting of profits. Theaters often intentionally blur your image on-screen in order to cut operating costs. Many stars visit movie theaters surreptitiously on their new picture's opening day, sneaking into the darkened theater just as the film begins. They are often shocked to look up and see that their image on the screen is blurred. The explanation for this horror: On a filmstrip, the best image occurs when the film passes close to the movie projector's high-powered lamp. But if it passes too closely, it can catch on fire. One person used to monitor each projector to prevent flames, but in a cost-cutting move, many cinema chains have assigned one projectionist to run as many as eight projectors at a time. For safety's sake, the projectionist sets the film a tiny bit farther away from the lamp. That prevents fires but makes you look fuzzy and indistinct.

WHAT AN AGENT DOES

Agents are curious figures in finely cut blue suits and white shirts who could easily be mistaken for FBI operatives who shop at Jil Sander. They often have cute names like Dave, Bruce, or Colin and can be found eating lunch in whichever dining rooms are of the moment, at the moment. At night they investigate star parties or lie in bed reading scripts and contracts. A good agent knows everything there is to know about budgets, directors, industry fights, and intimate gossip, based on intelligence gathered from making more than two hundred phone calls a day.

Here's the way a typical agent operates: The agent phones you asking for a piece of information. You refuse to divulge what you know. The agent threatens to ruin your reputation by finding the information out from someone else and then telling everyone in the industry that you were the one who leaked it. Faced with this threat, you'll probably cough up what the agent wants to know.

When they aren't threatening people, agents spend a lot of time in pursuit of big clients. They appear from nowhere at parties. They show up at the next table at your favorite restaurant. They become part of your life without you realizing it. Agents employ several tactics when seducing new star clients:

1. They offer to sign your brother, sister, and mother along with you.
2. They offer, confidentially, to take you on at no fee (it's worth it; having you as a client boosts their reputation and helps them draw other stars).

3. They promise to represent you themselves, with the utmost personal attention. Unfortunately, after signing with the agency, newbies are almost always handed over to lower-level agents.

No matter how the agent ropes you in, it's imperative that your agent at least pretends to respect and admire you. A good agent can earn you a lot of money. He'll merge your talents with other entities he represents, such as corporations, directors, and theme parks. Of course, he'll take a dime from every dollar you earn. He's expected to bring commissions worth three times his salary into the agency—super agents, of which there are about two dozen in Hollywood, earn more than $5 million a year. As should be obvious, he wants you just as much as you want him. Whether or not you like him makes no difference. Just smile, never forget to ask for more money than he's gotten you, and always be kind to the mailroom guys—they're the ones who read the scripts first.

STAR ISSUE: How to Fire an Agent

Step 1. Speak to your attorney.

Step 2. Make a deal with another agent. As a safeguard, you should never fire your agent before lining up the next one. But this can be tricky: As a professional courtesy, many agents will inform fellow agents that they are in the process of stealing their clients. Don't be surprised if emotions run high.

Step 3. Have your manager send your agent a good-bye e-mail or fax. Make sure it is kind, direct, and succinct.

Step 4. Make sure your attorney is protecting you.

Step 5. Tell your new agent you will never leave the new agency. Insist that you are loyal to a fault.

AVERAGE STAR SALARIES

Only three thousand of the more than one hundred thousand members of the Screen Actors Guild earn more than $1 million a year. Stars account for perhaps a few dozen of these. The world's top ten stars now earn more than thirty times what their counterparts earned in the 1940s, after correcting for inflation. Reflecting the state of society at large, male stars are paid more than female stars. For men, the $30-million-per-film mark has been broken, excluding ancillary profit arrangements. Female stars still struggle to break the $20-million barrier. Certainly, no male actor earning less than $15 million per film can truly be considered a star. The same applies for a female actor earning less than $12 million.

ANATOMY OF A MOVIE DEAL

"Not a half-dozen men have been able to keep the whole
equation of pictures in their heads."
—F. SCOTT FITZGERALD, *THE LAST TYCOON*

Stars have many revenue streams. For instance, a movie contract may address profits from many other entities than the movie itself, including video games, online games, comic books, TV spin-offs, clothes, toys, fast-food tie-ins, soundtrack recordings, DVDs, and more. But the standard star contract revolves around two types of deals:

Net Participation: The star gets a set percentage of the profits of the movie after it has broken even. Unfortunately, because studios are adept at making it look like their movies never break even, only 5 percent of films ever show a "profit." As it's nearly impossible to penetrate studio accounting practices, it's rare that a star profits from a net participation agreement. Don't sign one.

Gross Participation: The star gets a cut of the movie's gross earnings. Usually the cut kicks in after the film has earned a set amount, say $100 million. But the most powerful stars ask for "dollar one" participation, meaning their pockets begin to fill with the first dollar the film earns. Unfortunately for the less-powerful people who've signed net participation agreements, the money earned by stars with dollar-one gross participation is added on to the total production costs, making breaking even that much more of a pipe dream.

SAMPLE EARNINGS

One muscular action-picture star received the following deal. The negotiations took eighteen months, but the star was aided by the fact that the producers had already spent $20 million developing the script and securing the other stars for a project in which he was the irreplaceable centerpiece.

- Salary: $29.25 million
- Perks (jets, trailers, suites, limos, bodyguards): $1.5 million
- Gross participation from all sources (worldwide sales of DVDs, videos, licensing, theaters, and more): 20 percent

When some expensive scenes needed to be reshot during postproduction, this star showed his willingness to compromise and be a team player by taking a $3-million salary cut to defray costs. This boosted his image in the industry, and in the end, he earned more from the film than the studio did.

HOW TO JUSTIFY YOUR EXISTENCE

Often, people from the ROW don't understand or respect Hollywood celebrities. From their point of view, all stars are either lucky or they're sellouts—or even lucky sellouts. This can make nonindustry social functions and business gatherings difficult to maneuver. The following argument can protect you from the player haters (PHs) you encounter at cocktail parties: According to the theory of superstars postulated by the late economist Sherwin Rosen, one of the most striking aspects of the modern world is that in every industry, a small group of people tend to dominate their fields and earn huge amounts of money. (That would be you.) Writing in the *American Economic Review,* Rosen attributed the huge paychecks superstars collect to something called *allocative equilibrium,* in which small skill advances by superstars are rewarded disproportionately in a convex revenue function. This means that in our era, barely perceptible differences in talent are commonly magnified into much greater levels of success (i.e., your large private jet). This function is aided by the joint consumption technology (movie screens) that allows millions to observe, judge, and reward a star's performance however they see fit. This argument should be sufficient to disarm all citizens of the ROW that you are likely to encounter.

STAR KNOWLEDGE: Stop Dates

Stars are able to protect themselves from being overworked by introducing "stop dates" into their contracts. Such amendments stipulate that the star will work for six weeks only, beyond which they will need a substantial increase in pay. This means that if a film's production schedule extends past the contractual date, the star will receive a weekly lump sum to continue acting—$1.4 million per week is not unheard of.

BLOCKBUSTER

The term *blockbuster* was first used in the 1920s to describe a movie so popular that the ticket line was longer than a single block. Today, with tickets by phone and lines that meander back and forth within the Cineplex, the term is used to describe any hit movie.

THE BUDGET

All star movies have detailed budgets, with the average green-light commitment now hovering around $130 million. The following figures are from the 150-plus-page budget for a sequel to a successful action movie:

Art department: $1.2 million	*Extras: $500,000*
Camera crew: $2.5 million	*Film prints: $5 million*
Cast insurance: $2 million	*Film and processing: $1 million*
Completion bond: $2.5 million	*Legal and accounting: $2 million*
Digital effects: $20 million	*Lighting: $2.5 million*
Directors: $5 million	*Locations: $4.5 million*
Dubbing: $500,000	*Makeup: $500,000*
Editing: $2.5 million	*Music: $2 million*

Producers: *$10 million*
Production staff: *$2 million*
Publicity: *$45 million*
Script: *$2 million*
Second units: *$5.5 million*
Sets: *$12 million*
Sound: *$500,000*
Special effects: *$8 million*

Star: *$30 million*
Studio rental: *$2 million*
Stunts: *$1.5 million*
Titles: *$150,000*
Transportation: *$4 million*
Unforeseen expenses: *$7 million*
Wardrobe: *$1.5 million*
Total: $185.35 million

STUDIO ACCOUNTING PRACTICES

Stars should not feel guilty about extracting large sums of money from studios, because studios are extremely profitable, whether or not their official bottom line reflects these profits. Studios are well-known for creative accounting, and they do their Byzantine best to obscure financial realities (in their favor), using off-the-book corporations, pro forma (aka "wishful thinking") accounting, hedging operations, hidden salaries (through stock options), outsourced financing and production, and other creative methods. The studio revenue stream is more like a river with many tributaries, including:

Outside investors
Equity partners
Toy and other manufacturers
Fast-food outlets
Cinema chains
Airlines
Hotels
Distribution subsidiaries
DVD sales and rentals (the largest revenue tributary)
Television
Music DVDs
Digital downloads

The outflow of money is equally diversified, flowing to:

Payroll (one particular studio has seven thousand full-time employees)
Property rights (lease or purchase of copyright)
Talent (actors)
Producers
Film production (employees, equipment, food, lodging, transportation)
Film and processing
Insurance
Independent vendors such as computer graphics companies
Film prints ($1,500 per print, on average, for up to four thousand prints)
Advertising (domestic and overseas)
DVD production

SELLING OUT, DISCREETLY

Stars who do television advertisements in the United States for shaving cream, juice boxes, underwear, and other products are often seen as desperate, perhaps headed for bankruptcy. But stars can safely turn a quick profit doing commercials that will never air outside of Japan. Japanese consumers respond well to American star images in their advertisements, and ad agencies there will pay astronomical sums for a star shill (SS). Stars have flogged credit cards, sausages, coffee, whiskey, diamonds, beer, apple juice, face cream, and more. The shoots often take place in Los Angeles, so no travel is involved. One star was paid $2 million to go to an LA studio, dress as a detective, slurp a bowl of noodles, and capture a thief in a credit card commercial. Another earned more than $1 million to sit in a bathtub and share shampoo and body wash with a rubber ducky. These are just two examples of how stars can exploit their own charisma while retaining their self-respect.

STAR, INC.

Establishing a personal production company (PPC) is a smart way to defray personal expenses. A PPC is like a ministudio that finances deals, produces films, and generates huge amounts of income (or losses). Usually, the PPC is backed, in part, by at least one studio that gains an appreciable tax write-off from the arrangement. Many expenses that might otherwise be considered personal can be billed to the PPC and paid for with S&M. These include:

- Entourage members (hired as consultants)
- Mistresses and misters (hired as masseuses or trainers)
- Lawyers
- Script readers
- Bodyguards
- Pilots
- Chefs
- Trainers
- Transportation

PRODUCT BRANDING

Good managers and agents are ever vigilant for branding opportunities. The studios act as clearinghouses for the profits that come in from a wide variety of branded merchandise. A single big movie, especially one featuring mechanical or one-dimensional action figures (such as a dinosaur, alien killer, soldier, sexpot, or hero cop), can generate billions of dollars in income from theme-park rides, merchandise, candy, and clothes. Writers, producers, investors, and others will compete with you for a share of the studio's take. Fight for what you can get, but take heart: Even a small percentage, directed into your financial accounts, will ensure a comfortable retirement.

THE TWO BASIC HOLLYWOOD PATHS

FIRST MILLION ——————▶ MANY MILLIONS ——————▶ MANY MORE MILLIONS

FIRST MILLION ——————▶ MANY MILLIONS ——————▶ NO MILLIONS

STAR ISSUE: Fees

To stay big, you have to pay big. For every dollar you earn, you must pay the following people:

Agent: 10 cents

Manager: 10 to 20 cents

Publicity agent: 5 to 10 cents

Accountant: 5 cents

Conservative total: *30 cents of every dollar paid to essential employees, before taxes*

HOLLYWOOD SECRET: The Happy Mailbox

Stars never approach their mailbox with dread. At home, your mail will include only junk, newspapers and magazines, late-night online purchases, and the occasional thank-you note or personal letter. You will never receive a bothersome bill, legal document, invitation, check, or financial statement. The invitations will go to your publicist. The legal documents will go to your lawyer. And the financial statements, checks, and bills will go to your accountant. He will deposit your paychecks, pay all your bills, and invest the remaining money. When you want to obtain a new Bentley, house, or Cambodian orphan, your accountant will make all the arrangements, if he thinks you can afford it. The fan letters from people whose money pays for all these luxuries will be collected and answered by your PA.

ANNUAL STAR EXPENSES

Age-reversing antioxidant therapies: $24,000

Automotive detailer: $9,600 (three cars)

Automotive (miscellaneous): $36,000

Butler: $80,000

Caterer: $12,500

Chef: $75,000

Children's therapist: $6,500 (one child)

Dog walker: $16,425

Driver: $40,000

Entourage: $440,000

Erotic services: $24,000

Estate manager: $150,000

Exotic pet maintenance: $120,000

Gardener: $29,000

Gifts (business): $125,000

Gifts (personal): $8,000

Guru: $125,000

Health insurance: $24,000

Herbal mud therapy: $7,800

Home furnishings: $650,000

Hotels: $100,000 (not including comps)

Jet travel: $3 million (not including comps)

Las Vegas (weekends; inclusive of gambling, but not compulsive gambling): $950,000

Limousine: $360,000

Maid: $29,000

Mirrors: $68,000

Mortgage: $0 (cash purchase)

Nanny (round the clock): $164,259 (one child)
Nutraceuticals: $960
Organic produce and meat: $9,000 (one person)
Parties: $60,000 (excluding corporate sponsorship)
Personal assistant: $75,000
Pet grooming: $2,400
Pied-à-terre (rental): $36,000 (one lover)
Pool boy additional expenses (gifts): $20,000
Property manager: $120,000
Spa getaways: $25,000
Summer camp: $12,000 (one child)
Therapist: $13,000
Transportation (train, Greyhound, taxis): $45,000

Total: $7,092,444 or $19,431 per day

STAR KNOWLEDGE: Nonfinancial Remuneration

As a star, you will receive many unsolicited free products and services. Firms such as Backstage Creations work with corporations to "gift the talent" with tens of thousands of dollars worth of luxury goods. Don't feel guilty accepting these gifts—the companies are using you for publicity and account for such expenditures in their advertising budgets. Feel free to use the companies in return by having your publicist ask for anything you want—a car, a suit, a watch, a diamond necklace. Chances are you'll get it. In some cases they'll even pay you to accept these gifts. Clothing companies especially are known to pay stars six-figure sums to wear their creations.

HOLLYWOOD STOCK EXCHANGE

Stars, like sports heroes, are in the fortunate position of being able to bet on or against themselves. Several online gaming operations offer odds on when a star birth, wedding, breakup, rehab visit, or death will take place. The Hollywood Stock Exchange (http://movies.hsx.com) offers a virtual market in star careers. These can be easily manipulated from your end to improve your bottom line.

STAR ISSUE: Switching from Movies to Television

In the past, film stars felt TV was crass, commercial, and unartistic, unlike their own first-rate feature films. They'd snub their noses at television projects, appearing on TV only when it was necessary to promote their movies. This barrier prevented all but the most stalwart TV stars from crossing into celluloid fame. However, that stigma has lessened considerably in the last decade as cable channels have offered more enlightened and sophisticated programming. Money has also had a powerful reverse effect on snobbery. Reality TV shows based on stars' lives bring in huge amounts of money and promise further vast sums in the residual market. This is especially attractive to aging stars afraid that their light is about to dim.

HOLLYWOOD SECRET: The Black Card

Stars often find that their platinum cards aren't capable of easily absorbing large purchases, such as a convertible Maybach or the charter of a private jet. To help people of means avoid lengthy phone calls with the credit card company, American Express offers the Black Card (officially known as the Centurion Card) to members who generally charge more than $150,000 per year. The $2,500 annual fee gives you access to free airline upgrades, membership in airport VIP lounges and travel services, advice on gifts, and telephone advice on everything from horoscopes to the best bulimia treatment centers. Plus, you can charge even the most expensive items without fear of rejection. There is no application process: The company will contact you.

THE GOLDEN STATUE

Some stars feel ashamed of how badly they want to win an Oscar, as though it indicates how badly their egos need to be stroked. But this burning desire can also have very practical financial implications for star and studio. According to the scholarly work "What's an Oscar Worth?" by Randy Nelson and associates, published in the journal *Economic Inquiry*, Oscars benefit the bottom line. Using a series of complex mathematical calculations, Nelson determined that just being nominated for an Oscar increased the theatrical run of a movie by an average of 117 percent. A nomination for best actress or actor increased the number of screens showing the film by 41.16 percent. *Winning* best actress or actor increased the number of screens by 122.32 percent. The nominees for best picture saw

PREDICTED VALUES OF AN OSCAR NOMINATION AND AWARD

	RELEASE DATE			
	1st Quarter	2nd Quarter	3rd Quarter	4th Quarter
Best Actress/ Actor Nomination	13%	7%	19%	61%
Award	20%	0%	15%	65%
Best Picture Nomination	18%	8%	20%	54%
Award	0%	0%	33%	67%

By Randy Nelson et al, from *Economic Inquiry*, January 2001, vol. 39, no.1, pp. 1–6(6), published by Oxford University Press. Estimates adjusted for probability of survival.

their screen count rise by 84.95 percent. And the winners gained 200.76 percent more screens. The length of a run and the number of screens both influence the earnings of a film. The "Predicted Values of an Oscar Nomination and Award" table illustrates the percentage increase in earnings as a result of various nominations and awards.

WHAT IS AN OSCAR?

- The Academy of Motion Picture Arts and Sciences "statue of merit" is known as the Oscar because an Academy librarian once said it looked like her uncle Oscar.
- The figure shows a sword-wielding knight propped on a reel of film with five radiating spokes that signify the original branches of the academy: actors, writers, directors, producers, and technicians.
- Oscar is cast brittanium—an alloy similar to pewter—plated with layers of copper, nickel, silver, and 24-karat gold.
- It stands 13.5 inches tall, weighs 8.5 pounds, and has a basic value of $330.
- All recipients must sign a waver promising never to sell their statues.
- It takes twelve employees of R. S. Owens, a Chicago company, to make each statue.
- R. S. Owens has repaired more than 160 damaged statues over the years, due to falls or zealous housekeepers wielding chemical polishes.

OSCAR SWAG

Nominees at the Oscars are presented with gift bags valued at more than $1 million, provided by companies that desire to associate their products with stars. While some ceremonies offer rooms full of stuff that celebrities and barnacles can paw through, taking what they want in an orgy of gift porn (GP), the Oscars remain tasteful. While you might be asked to pose backstage for photographs of you and your products, feel free to refuse this offer of mutual exploitation. And take the bag, anyway—it's your right as a star. It's considerate to give anything you don't like to your maid. Some recent swag included:

- $1,500 party at Morton's Steakhouse
- $14,000 in hotel stays at Small Luxury Hotels of the World
- $6,000 wide-screen digital television
- $540 in Armando Manni olive oil
- $3,200 Tahitian pearl necklace
- $700 Krups kitchen set
- $600 red leather case with makeup and mink eyelashes
- $500 cashmere pajama bottoms
- $3,500 day of spa services
- $350 worth of chocolate truffles in a Waterford vase
- $3,000 vacation in Cabo San Lucas
- $250 writing pen
- $1,000 Fendi watch

✦✦✦

CHAPTER 7

LEISURE

SUCCESSFUL RELAXATION
REQUIRES A LOT OF WORK

EVEN STARS NEED A BREAK

A single movie can consume six straight weeks of days that begin with the star climbing into the limousine after breakfast and not returning home until dinner with time in between, perhaps, for only one short nap. The star spends much of the day in an exhausting attempt to delve deeply into his or her soul for emotional responses to comic situations, and vice versa, before collapsing in the three-bedroom hotel suite supplied by the studio. Even with the services of a personal chef, the food somehow always tastes different from home. On top of everything, the attention from stylists, makeup artists, other crew members, and the director is constant. Stress can rise to unimagined levels.

Clearly, a star needs a break after making a movie. But the star faces special leisure conditions unknown to people in the ROW. Even in remote, expensive, and well-insulated locales, the star inevitably runs the risk of encountering SFs, CUs, ERs, FSFs, ACJs, and IPs who are out for a piece of the star's image. In day-to-day leisure activities, such as bowling, a star must create a bubble of tranquillity, built from syco-phants, bodyguards, or velvet rope, simply in order to relax. The star has certain career obligations—exquisite attention to public image, pri-marily—that make leisure time a serious undertaking. A grand leading lady caught schussing at Aspen in a mismatched ski suit will find her disgraced image exposed in the gossip pages of the morning paper. Those who ignore this fact and expose their foibles, ugly sides, or recent weight gain to the public suffer possibly permanent reductions of SP. So, as a star, you must be willing to pay dearly for privacy. When in public, take care to carefully choreograph your fun, and always look good for the cameras—if your SP hasn't faded, there will always be one within range.

STAR KNOWLEDGE: Bowling

Bowling promotes physical fitness and healthy relationships, and it lets stars connect with two important demographics: regular Joes and casual hipsters. Lucky Strike Lanes, at the intersection of Hollywood Boule-vard and Highland Avenue, is the place where stars prefer to roll all of their splits, strikes, and gutter balls. This is an intimate, upscale alley, befitting your status, and it features a bar, restaurant, party room, and floor-to-ceiling video screens behind the pins. You will be noticed if you bowl here. Lessons and rentals are available, but you should always bring your own shoes to avoid picking up a fungus from the ROW's feet.

Some Bowling Tips

Keep your arm loose
Bend at the knee before releasing the ball
Loft ball over foul line
Use creative visualization to imagine yourself winning
Watch professional bowlers on TV
Hire a stunt double to bowl for you

HOLLYWOOD SECRET: Shop Naked

Like all Americans, stars love to shop. But for some stars, having to face SFs and RPs with autograph pens makes shopping on Rodeo Drive, Robertson Boulevard, or even at Fred Siegel a tedious experience. While many LA boutiques will offer the courtesy of locking the front door to let the star shop unmolested, there's nothing to prevent fans and paparazzi from gathering on the sidewalk to stare and leave affectionate paw and lip prints on the window. To avoid this, many stars resort to shopping in their living rooms:

- Page through a fashion magazine. If something strikes your fancy, call the fashion design house and ask the publicist to send over the item in your size, for free. Don't worry, they'll comply.

- Call any boutique or store in Los Angeles and tell them more or less what you are looking for. Within hours, a crate of clothing will be delivered to your home. Try on items to your heart's content. Keep what you'd like, and throw the rest on the floor. The store will retrieve it, and your accountant will get the bill.

STAR ISSUE: Buyer Beware

While shopping is very pleasurable for most stars, it can become a dangerous addiction for others when used to assuage emotional inadequacies and low self-esteem. Psychologists say that a complex chemical exchange is probably at the heart of shopping addiction. Watching your personal shopper select shiny items causes your body to release a calming chemical called *serotonin* into your brain. As the serotonin rushes in, anxiety and depression rush out. But within a matter of minutes, as you are piloting your Jaguar onto Rodeo Drive, the problems of the world return to wash the beauty of your purchases away, and you begin to sink inevitably back into a pit of anxiety, depression, alienation, and ugliness that not even a gross-profit-participation contract could counter.

The *Diagnostic and Statistical Manual of Mental Disorders* of the American Psychiatric Association doesn't have a separate category for compulsive shopping. But this ailment fits neatly into the general category of "Impulse-Control Disorders, Not Otherwise Specified."

For these types of disorders, awareness is the first step in controlling the problem. Try to notice those moments when your shopping gets out of control—most likely when you feel like a failed negative person (FNP). Take pains to understand your habits and get comfortable with the idea of changing them. Take a month or so to let it settle in; then it's time to take the following steps to minimize the damage.

- Set standards limiting what you can and can't buy—be realistic but strict.
- Don't let one binge lead to another. A shopping binge is just a mistake, not a verdict on your future. Start fresh after each one.
- Become aware of what you're doing when you get the urge to binge; chances are that you have certain triggers, such as a bad PR campaign, a bad review, or an absent pool boy.
- When those moods strike, go for a walk, read a book, or watch TV. Don't go living room shopping.
- See a therapist to find out why you shop the way you do.
- When all else fails, take drugs.

Scientists haven't devoted the same efforts to curing compulsive shopping that they have to eradicating major diseases like diabetes, but a few brave researchers are working to free shopaholics from their demons. At Stanford University, compulsive shoppers have successfully been calmed with selective serotonin reuptake inhibitors (SSRIs), the kind of pills your fellow stars may take to cure ennui. These drugs encourage serotonin to enter and stay in the brain longer. Dr. Lorrin Koran, a professor of psychiatry and director of Stanford's Obsessive-Compulsive Disorder Clinic, says compulsive shopping hits women nine times more often than men. To test the effects of SSRI drugs, he gave a group of nineteen women and two men a common SSRI called citalopram (Celexa) at 20 mg a day to start. The dose was increased as needed if a test subject showed no improvement. After just twelve weeks, the patients reported far less shopping overall. Yet another Stanford researcher has found that 80 percent of compulsive shoppers who took citalopram improved "markedly." In other words, the drug works. Your doctor can prescribe it.

STAR SUPERFANS

Attending a Los Angeles Lakers game gives the star a unique peek inside the SF lifestyle, as the star is expected to clap, shout, and spill food right along with the ROW. It also helps counter homophobic rumors and lets you mingle with influential IPs. However, given that stars are regularly featured on the game's network broadcasts and on the arena's Jumbotron, sitting in a less-than-prestigious seat can seriously damage a star's career. Season tickets are sold out years in advance and are nearly impossible to secure on short notice. More occasional star SFs must work the system to secure house seats. Unfortunately, since the sports world operates in a different universe than the star world, you can't just call up and demand seats based on your Hollywood wattage. Here are tips for getting the proper view:

- Before calling for tickets, bone up on the game, so you appear to actually know something about basketball, rather than coming across as someone who is just looking to network with IPs.
- Ask your studio or agency for any extra tickets they might have.
- Work through the Lakers's director of sales and marketing, who controls the house seats.
- Make the calls yourself. Having your publicist call marks you as an arrogant fool. The Lakers don't like to be pushed around.
- Be willing to pay up to $1,900 per seat ($2,800 for finals). Do not ask for comps.
- Ask for a Chairman's Room pass, which allows you entrance to a private lounge during halftime, where you can talk rock (basketball) with fellow stars.
- Don't ask for special parking privileges.
- Don't get drunk or stoned and wander onto the court to advise the players on their game.

FOREIGN ESCAPES

While DVDs and videos spread your charisma to the farthest corners of the earth, there are eight countries where your SP is most evident, simply because they show the most Hollywood films. The risk of being harassed by a foreign superfan (FSF) is greatest in the following places (in descending order based on annual theater showings of American films):

Japan

Germany

Britain

Spain

France

Australia

Italy

Mexico

FLYING COMMERCIAL

At times, studios balk at providing a private jet for a star's leisure travel. The star has the choice of throwing a fit, and possibly ruining her vacation, or flying commercial. Surprisingly, with airlines introducing improved first-class cabins, the experience has become more enjoyable lately, with perks such as:

- Copper espresso machines
- Complimentary facials and haircuts
- Freshly prepared salads
- Custom cocktails
- Accoustic-noise-canceling headsets
- Krug and Taittinger Comtes de Champagne

- Free designer ties
- Shanghai Tang sleeper suits
- Osetra caviar
- One attendant for every four passengers
- Personal toasters for do-it-yourself breakfast
- Onboard showers
- Free crayons
- Built-in seat massagers and room-service phones
- Vanity mirrors
- E-mail
- Personal minibars
- Flight attendants who perform magic tricks; address passengers by name; form onboard choirs or string quartets; remember personal wine, film, magazine, and conversation preferences; smile, even when passengers are rude; clean the toilet after each use

STAR-CLASS SEATING

It can be tiresome to sit upright during a commercial flight. To avoid back pain, choose an airline with seats that turn into a bed. Emirates Airline offers fully enclosed first-class cabins, with fully reclining seats, much like in a luxury train compartment. But it's not often that stars fly to Dubai.

Before booking seats on other airlines, be sure they offer one of these two seat types:

Lie-flat: seats that lie flat, at an angle
Flat bed: seats that recline to full flat position

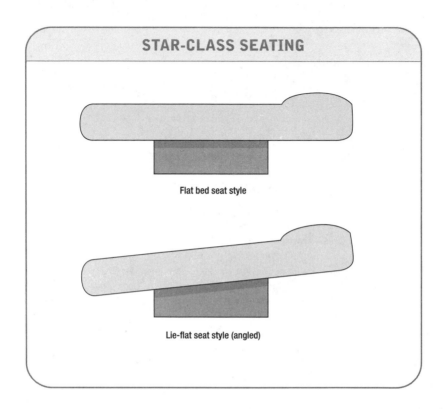

STAR-CLASS SEATING

Flat bed seat style

Lie-flat seat style (angled)

STAR KNOWLEDGE: The World's Most Expensive Lunch

A sure test of star status is a lunch reservation at the Eagle restaurant, in the ski resort of Gstaad, Switzerland. The Eagle is a members-only restaurant that does not accept applications. Even after being invited to join, some people wait up to three years for a reservation and spend many thousands of dollars in the process. You, however, might be able to eat sooner, and for less, by trading on star power. Instruct your publicist to keep your reservation campaign tasteful and low key by working through existing members. It's not unusual to see several kings and a couple of queens at lunch, which, very reasonably, runs under $100 (in addition to the $25,000 membership fee). But the presence of a true star livens up a dining room in the way that simple royalty often can't. Expect an invitation soon.

PROS AND CONS: Private Vacations vs. Media Circus Vacations

PRIVATE VACATIONS

Are relaxing

Promote intimacy with loved ones

Are healthy for your body and soul

Clear your mind

Give you a new perspective on the unreality of your life

Promote spiritual discovery

MEDIA CIRCUS VACATIONS

Help your career

Help loved one's career

Are healthy for your bank account

Fill your publicity clip file

Inflate your ego and make you feel even more important

Confirm your status as a demigod

VACATION LOCALES

PRIVATE

Mustique

Gstaad

Wyoming ranch

Lake Como

Loire Valley Château

Costa Rican surfing school

Shelter Island

Tobago

Kansas Flint Hills

The Sudan

PUBLIC

Miami Beach

Aspen

Wyoming State Fair

Lake of the Ozarks

Eiffel Tower and the Louvre

Coney Island

Easthampton

St. Barts

Notting Hill, London

Las Vegas

DOS AND DON'TS: Leisure Wardrobe

The typical star leisure wardrobe is a pathetic thing to behold. It's your obligation to improve this aspect of star life. Never wear:

Terry cloth beach wraps with bikini tops
Low-slung surfer shorts
Mandals (leather men's sandals)
Tattoo-exposing wife beaters
Expensive Fred Siegel T-shirts with ironic messages
Velour tracksuits
Giant basketball sneakers
Trucker caps
Biker wallet chains
Naval rings
Male sarongs (if you are overweight)

COLLECTING ART

Hollywood is populated by frustrated artists. Screenwriters who want to be novelists. Scenic artists who want to show in galleries. Soundtrack composers who wish they were writing for the London Symphony Orchestra. At times a star may feel compelled to lose an ear just to be validated. Avoid falling into this trap. Being a star is good enough. And it gives you the money to collect the work of other artistes, which is among the most pleasurable leisure activities in Hollywood. Collecting art gives a star intellectual cachet and opens doors to highbrow parties at the Museum of Contemporary Art, the Los Angeles County Museum of Art, and the Getty Center, where you can avoid the SFs who might accost you during regular museum hours. You can either immerse yourself in art history or hire an art consultant to do the thinking for you. As a precautionary measure, always have the consultant make your purchases. When a star walks into a gallery, dollar signs appear in the staff's eyes; a consultant can get you a more realistic price and a better match for your décor. Collecting art is at least as expensive as collecting vintage automobiles, and entry-level high-quality work often costs hundreds of thousands of dollars. Fortunately, there's no longer any reason to suffer with difficult paintings. Today's most popular star artists make art that's very easy to grasp and pleasing to the eye.

ARTIST	STYLE
John Currin	*Soft-core and scary old-school porn*
Eric Fischl	*A Goya for angst-ridden yuppies driven to excess*
Takashi Murakami	*Reminds you of stuff you'd like to find in children's cereal boxes*
Ed Ruscha	*Paints words, rather than pictures; limited vocabulary but good spelling*
Lisa Yuskavage	*Boobs, butts, and bellies make up her oversize pornographic greeting cards*
Raymond Pettibon	*Really excellent doodles*
Cecily Brown	*Colorful and gloppy abstract paintings by an artist who is famous for her own extravagant lips*
Gabriel Orozco	*Photographs with Spanish titles that will interest your maid*
Gregory Crewdson	*Still photos of elaborate sets that are as pretentious as any Hollywood movie production*
Cindy Sherman	*She makes herself up, just like you do, and then takes her own portrait*
Sam Taylor-Wood	*Photographs of very cool-looking people who you'd like to meet, in cool-looking places that you'd like to own*
Thomas Ruff	*Photographs of other people's porno websites*

STAR ISSUE: Kidnapping

It's a fact. People all over the world know you are rich, and they are willing to kidnap you or your loved ones for money. This is most likely to happen when you are on vacation, especially overseas. There, language barriers might make it difficult to understand the kidnappers' demands, but eventually you'll figure out that they're asking for more than an autograph. This is where emergency help can come in handy. Control Risk Groups (CRG) is a leading crisis response services provider that consults with businesses and individuals on how to prevent or respond to kidnappings. If you are subject to a kidnapping, CRG will dispatch someone to your side within twenty-four hours to assist the victim and deal with family, employees, governments, law enforcement, and the media. The company brings structure to chaotic situations. According to CRG, these are the best ways to prevent a kidnapping:

Analyze the risk in the country you are visiting

Take thorough security precautions

Survey buildings where you will be staying

Travel with bodyguards

Send your chauffeur to defensive driving school

Have contingency plans for various kidnapping situations

Prepare yourself for what happens during a kidnapping to reduce your fear

If you or someone you know is kidnapped, CRG suggests that you immediately hire a consultant to:

Evaluate the circumstances and outline options

Tell you how to negotiate

Coordinate the various interested parties' responses

Help the victim after he or she is released

STAR RISKS

Each year the world becomes more dangerous for traveling stars, according to the Global Filmmaking Map published by Aon/Albert G. Ruben, an insurance broker for the entertainment industry. The map lists ninety-one high-risk countries and twenty-one very-high-risk countries for people in the film industry. The greatest risk is from disease, followed by poor medical care, crime, terrorism, political instability, organized crime and corruption, and kidnapping and ransom. Popular star destinations such as Mexico, Thailand, the Philippines, and South Africa are very risky now and should be avoided.

YACHTS

Yachts offer privacy, safety, and prestige to the star in search of relaxation. When the quiet of the open seas becomes too much to bear, the yacht can pull into a magnificent port where other stars, IPs, and media titans are practicing their leisure skills. It is rare for a star to maintain a large yacht, given that they are usually used for fewer than three weeks a year. However, fabulous charters are easy to find, at prices ranging from $350,000 to $850,000 per week, plus 20 percent tip for the crew. Stars may choose from a "megayacht" or "superyacht" that is more than eighty feet long, or from a "really big yacht" that's more than one hundred fifty feet stem to stern. The typical vacation schedule on a yacht is as follows:

10:00 A.M.–noon	*Breakfast on a shaded deck*
noon–2:00 P.M.	*Lunch poolside*
2:00 P.M.–8:00 P.M.	*Rest, movies, and fun with special friends in private stateroom*
8:00 P.M.–midnight	*Dinner in the stateroom*
Midnight–dawn	*Drinking, dancing, and carrying on all over the yacht*

"CHRISTINA O" YACHT

COMPASS DECK

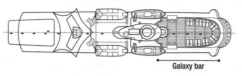

Galaxy bar

BRIDGE DECK

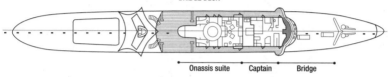

Onassis suite   Captain   Bridge

PROMENADE DECK

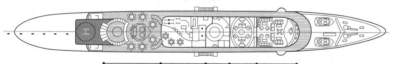

Jacuzzi deck   Sports lounge   Atrium   Library   Show lounge

MAIN DECK

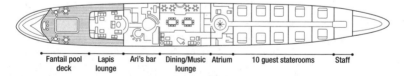

Fantail pool deck   Lapis lounge   Ari's bar   Dining/Music lounge   Atrium   10 guest staterooms   Staff

CABIN DECK

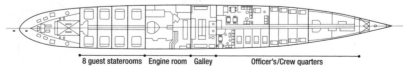

8 guest staterooms   Engine room   Galley   Officer's/Crew quarters

THE STAR YACHT

The schematics of a typical star yacht shown on the opposite page depict the layout of the bedrooms, galleys, party areas, and crew quarters.

PAPARAZZI CONTROL AT SEA

Yacht crews are trained to spot suspicious craft and warn stars—who are nude, poorly dressed, or in a compromising position—that paparazzi may be approaching. But it's more difficult to spot invaders who arrive under cover of darkness. To prevent unwanted photographs, the wise star will insist on the antipaparazzi system produced by the German design firm mylk* (*+49 [ø] 40-284076-60;* www.mylk.de). The system is based on highly directional and bright laser lights that shine a powerful beam into the lenses of pesky photographers on boats or onshore without disturbing passengers on board. The lights can be set to activate with motion detectors or can be turned on manually by a crew member.

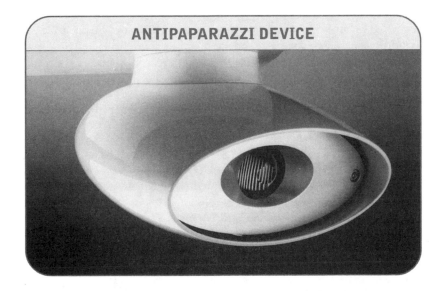

ANTIPAPARAZZI DEVICE

CHAPTER 8

TAKING A BOW
LIFE AND DEATH ISSUES

ILLUMINATE YOUR FADING STAR

The record life span for an RP is 122 years. The longest life span for a star is hard to quantify, because most fudge their birth dates, lift their faces, and dress a bit teenile. But stars do age. And they do die. Hollywood is a young person's world, and it behooves you to plan for the darkness that inevitably descends, in some form, on every star career. Planning for your forties, fifties, and beyond takes foresight and chutzpah. But if you're careful, you will remain a star well beyond the grave.

STAR ISSUE: Life Span

Stars must be careful not to reveal too much about their life progress. Follow these guidelines when discussing your age:

ACTUAL AGE	STATED AGE	ACTUAL AGE	STATED AGE
17	19	38	32
18	19	39	32
19	19	40	33
20	20	41	34
21	21	42	35
22	22	43	36
23	23	44	37
24	23	45	38
25	23	46	39
26	24	47	39
27	25	48	40
28	25	49	40
29	26	50	41
30	27	51	42
31	27	52	43
32	27	53	44
33	28	54	45
34	29	55	45
35	30	56	46
36	31	57	47
37	31	58	47

ACTUAL AGE	STATED AGE
59	*48*
60	*49*
61	*50*
62	*51*
63	*52*
64	*53*
65	*54*
66	*Don't discuss your age*
67	*Don't discuss your age*
68	*Don't discuss your age*
69	*Don't discuss your age*
70	*Don't discuss your age*
71	*Don't discuss your age*
72	*Don't discuss your age*
73	*Don't discuss your age*
74	*Don't discuss your age*
75	*From now on, proudly proclaim your true age*

THE WISDOM OF *SUNSET BOULEVARD*

The movie *Sunset Boulevard* is a cautionary tale for any star. Directed in 1950 by Billy Wilder, this classic film tells the story of Norma Desmond, a washed-up silent-screen star living alone in a mansion. Pacing the dimly lit rooms, she concocts a scheme to stage a comeback. "I'm big," she says. "It's the pictures that got small." Aided by the cynical machinations of a downtrodden screenwriter, she plots her return to stardom. Together they write a script for famed director Cecil DeMille. Gradually, her fantasies evaporate, and she shoots the screenwriter for deceiving her. That evening she loses her mind. In the morning, she hallucinates that she's back at the studio, a working actress. Her butler plays along with it, pretending to be DeMille directing her in a scene. As she descends the staircase of her musty mansion, she stops and tells him she can't go on with the scene because she's too happy. She promises to never abandon her fans again. The movie ends with Miss Desmond staring into the camera to utter the legendary line: "And now, Mr. DeMille, I'm ready for my close-up." This classic movie offers three valuable lessons for stars:

- Careers end
- Play your cards right and you'll end up with a mansion
- Don't trust screenwriters

HOLLYWOOD SECRET: A Living Legacy

Modern stars can greatly benefit from computer technology. Their age lines and love handles can be digitally erased, if necessary. And with motion capture (a technology originally developed to analyze the movements of cerebral palsy patients) and other software, they can continue to be stars from beyond the grave. The process is very expensive. The actor is fitted with special suits and marked with dots that the computer can use to plot a record of every nuanced movement. These digital files can later be used to invent any character imaginable, male or female, based on the star's natural shape and movement. With this information, a star can continue to appear in films for eternity.

STAR ISSUE: Failure

Not all careers last. Riches can be fleeting, and friends and publicists tend to disappear. Keep these numbers of homeless services in Hollywood handy:

Angels Flight Drop-In Center	*(800) 833-2499*
Children of the Night	*(818) 908-4474*
Covenant House	*(323) 461-3131*
Gay & Lesbian Community Services Center	*(323) 993-7400*
Los Angeles Free Clinic	*(323) 653-1990*
Los Angeles Youth Network	*(323) 957-7364*
My Friend's Place	*(323) 908-0011*
Salvation Army	*(323) 469-2946*
Teen Canteen	*(323) 468-2500*

STAR CEMETERY

The Hollywood Forever Cemetery is home to hundreds of celebrity corpses, both in mausoleums and underground. Established in 1899, it is the oldest cemetery in Hollywood, with acres of green grass dotted with lakes and towering palm trees. There are two large mausoleums with marble interiors and stained-glass windows, and several unusual monuments dot the parklike grounds, including obelisks and rocket ships. Burial plots are available at prices ranging from $1,000 for a simple site to $55,000 for a prime location near other stars. The flower shop sells maps of the cemetery and stars' graves. One day, if you're lucky, you will be included as well.

STAR DEPARTURE

Perhaps no star will ever depart this earth with the dignity and publicity afforded actor Ronald Reagan, who focused his star power to such an extent that at the end of a long, rich life, he drew every famous person on earth to his parting. But Ronald Reagan's funeral was not a haphazard event. His family and protectors met every year in the final decade of his life to plan the funeral details, including the timing of the sunset over the

Pacific as he was laid to rest. You, too, should plan carefully for your eventual departure from Hollywood. These seven tips for planning a funeral, from the United States Federal Trade Commission, should help:

Shop around for coffins, graves, funeral homes, and morticians

Get a price list for each service

Don't give in when pressured to buy services you don't want

Avoid spending too much just because you don't like contemplating what you're actually shopping for

Know the laws regarding burials, caskets, and services

Plan ahead

To which any star should add:

Prepay your publicist

Have a set designer sketch your mausoleum or monument

Keep the casket closed to protect your image

Have the service on the weekend, when sentimental news rules the airways

Set up a "fresh flower" trust in your will to ensure that your grave will be decorated with sweet-smelling arrangements in perpetuity

Insist that everyone refer to your funeral as your "grand finale"

STAR KNOWLEDGE: Death Notices

Have your executor notify the Popped Clogs Department of the *London News Review* (www.lnreview.co.uk/clogs). They dispatch e-mails to sub-scribers when anyone famous dies.

TEN APPROPRIATE STAR EPITAPHS

She made millions from millions

Happy starlet, early blest
Now in peaceful slumber, rest

She's left her rabid superfans
Her jet, bodyguard, and Mercedes-Benz
But heaven holds a place for her
With harps and God as her chauffeur

Thank God, I won't need antioxidants in heaven

This famous star had surgery
For improvements she thought necessary
In heaven they'll give her a poke
And ask why she fixed things that never were broke

With movie tie-ins and profit points
This star burned bright on this green earth
His family gladly now appoints
A lawyer to gauge his vast net worth

Digitized, he lives eternal

Look for me in the largest star trailer in heaven

She died long after her career

I was somebody

Mourn me not, instead go home
Turn off the ringer on the phone
Grab some chips and a DVD
Soon you'll see me on TV

♦♦♦

1. What is a four-band cell phone?

A. A party line shared by four rock groups

B. A cell phone with four decorative stripes to match your clothes

C. A phone that works in every country in the world

2. Define *majordomo.*

A. Military speak for a major who does more

B. The head butler or steward of a household

C. A type of very large, illegal sex toy

3. What do they say about pool technicians, aka "pool boys"?

A. With one look, they know exactly what your system needs

B. They will schedule visits at your pleasure

C. They know just how to fill a diva's pool

4. Is it possible to become a breeder without losing your girlish figure?

A. No. Just look around at all the flabby asses at the mall.

B. No. Just look at all the fat cows at any farm.

C. Yes. All you have to do is schedule preemptive surgical birthing, followed immediately by a tummy tuck.

5. What is the Hollywood definition of "home cooked"?

A. A meal prepared by a chef and served in your dining room

B. A meal you cook yourself (just kidding!)

C. Rock cocaine that has been prepared at home

6. Which of the following is *not* a problem at star dog runs?

A. B-level dog feces

B. Gawkers, stalkers, and low-class dog walkers

C. Canine STDs

7. Where have stars not been caught having sex in a "gronge" situation?

A. The men's restroom of Will Rogers Memorial Park
B. In a white luxury SUV just off Sunset Boulevard
C. In the privacy of a hotel suite with a date arranged in confidentiality by the star's agent

8. What is wardriving?

A. Renting a car for a drive through Iraq
B. A typical afternoon on the LA freeways
C. Cruising through celebrity neighborhoods with laptops trying to hack into signals from stars' wireless bedroom cameras

9. Define *gynecomastia.*

A. Bitch tits
B. Fear of gynecologists
C. A new protein drink, with special Amazon berry antioxidants

10. How can you make your ass an asset?

A. Hide it by wearing only vertical stripes
B. Flaunt it and make it your signature body part
C. Rent advertising space on each cheek

11. Which amenity is *not* commonly found in star substance-abuse rehabs?

A. Gourmet chef
B. Lap dancers
C. Juice bar

12. How is religion useful to a Hollywood star?

A. It provides a suitably supreme role model
B. It offers good plotlines and PR
C. It encourages humility

13. What is "the truth"?

A. The name of that new nightclub on the roof of that new hotel on Sunset, the one with beds instead of couches
B. The name of that new English rapper
C. The malleable concept that has been refined in sublime ways by postmodern public relations agents

14. Why do stars fall in love?

A. Pheromones
B. Drawn to money and power
C. As a way of promoting their latest movie

15. Can a star be gay?

A. No
B. You've got to be kidding
C. No, unless they meet the following criteria: sexy, adorable, lipstick-wearing, and female

16. When do politics and fame mix?

A. Never
B. Not ever
C. Not even sometimes

17. Describe the relationship between the journalist and the star.

A. Symbiotic
B. Parasitic
C. Professional

18. Which of the following pairs should never attempt an air kiss?

A. A nonstar and a nonstar
B. A gay man and an uncomfortably latent homosexual man
C. A closeted gay leading man and a closeted gay action hero star

19. *Paparazzi* is Italian for _____.

A. "buzzing insects"

B. "noodles in the shape of little Ferraris"

C. "you look gorgeous — can I take you home to meet my mother?"

20. On set, what behavioral trait is most important for a star?

A. Brilliance

B. Artistic genius

C. Good work ethic

21. What does it feel like to do all those dangerous moves, like walking on airplane wings, rappelling down buildings, and swimming with mad sharks?

A. Scary but fulfilling

B. Makes you proud of playing such an important role in entertaining bored Americans

C. Who knows? The insurance companies won't let stars do anything dangerous on set. Ask a stunt double.

22. Which of the following is *not* in your personal assistant's job description?

A. Cleaning your toenails

B. Dropping your stool samples at the lab

C. Walking your ferret

23. Who writes your screenplays?

A. The writer

B. Why should I care?

C. The director, I think

24. Movies usually run under two hours. Why?

A. That seems to be the best length for expressing artistic thoughts on the screen
B. Directors like to save film so there will be plenty for up-and-coming auteurs to use
C. Short films help popcorn sales

25. Thiruvananthapuram is the name of what?

A. A town in India noted for its rice dough string hoppers and a film festival
B. The self-help guru favored by young Hollywood
C. A rejuvenating amino acid found in llama fetuses

26. Private jets are fun, fast, and prestigious. But they also help an actor develop his craft (or art, depending on the actor). How?

A. You can fly to acting classes and get there real quick
B. They allow you to travel the world and meet people on which you can base your screen characters
C. They allow you to work on several movies at a time, jetting to and fro from here to there

27. What is the first step to take when preparing to perform an on-screen kiss?

A. Ask your makeup artist to examine the other person's mouth for any oral herpes sores
B. Apply your favorite lip gloss
C. Wink alluringly and give a little shake of your ass

28. When someone asks you how it feels to earn hundreds of millions of dollars, how do you reply?

A. "Man, it feels really f'in awesome!"
B. "Like shootin' rats with a machine gun!"
C. "The money is nice, of course, but in truth I am not in it for fame or riches. I'm in it for the art, for the chance to connect with millions, and in that way serve my God."

29. Agents could be mistaken for which type of person?

A. Fry cooks
B. Street hustlers
C. FBI agents

30. What is a good salary?

A. $19.99 per hour
B. Six figures, bro
C. $29 million, plus 20 percent of the gross, plus perks

31. According to the late economist Sherwin Rosen, why do some stars make so much dough?

A. It doesn't matter why; it just matters that you can drop an economist's name at cocktail parties
B. Because stars are brilliant, beautiful people deserving of adoration
C. Because inside every star is an avaricious fraud

32. How much does it cost to make movies?

A. A lot and then some
B. About $130 million
C. About the same as Bill Gates's house

33. Stars have happy mailboxes. Why?

A. They are filled with prescription painkillers ordered over the Internet
B. They hire people to sit inside them and smile when the star comes to collect the mail
C. They never receive bills, because their accountant takes care of that

34. Where did the gold statuettes at the Academy Awards get their name?

A. Oscar Schindler
B. Open Source Cluster Application Resources, the computer software that chooses the winners
C. It was the name of the uncle of one of the Academy librarians

35. Can a star be addicted to shopping?

A. No. Why do you ask?
B. Yes, and Stanford researchers use drugs to treat it
C. Not if you hire someone else to do it for you

36. Which country does not have a lot of superfans?

A. Britain
B. Suriname
C. Spain

37. When does the day begin on a chartered luxury yacht?

A. 7:00 A.M.
B. 7:30 A.M.
C. Whenever the hell you wake up!

38. What are the biggest dangers facing stars in foreign countries?

A. Disease
B. Kidnapping
C. America-loving teenagers with bad makeup

39. Star lives end in funerals. How should you prepare?

A. Prepay your publicist
B. Shop around for caskets
C. Sketch the design for your mausoleum or monument

40. Which of the following is an appropriate star epitaph?

A. Plastic surgery didn't help in the end
B. Her real name was Irena Mestlivachomic
C. She died before her time

KEY

35–40 correct answers: You are a star
20–34 correct answers: B list
0–19 correct answers: Go back to Kansas

1. C	**21.** C
2. B	**22.** A (you have a pedicurist to do that)
3. All of the above	**23.** B
4. C	**24.** C
5. A	**25.** A
6. C	**26.** B
7. C	**27.** A
8. C	**28.** C
9. A	**29.** C
10. B	**30.** C
11. B	**31.** A
12. B	**32.** All of the above
13. C	**33.** C
14. All of the above	**34.** C
15. C	**35.** B
16. All of the above	**36.** B
17. B	**37.** C
18. All of the above	**38.** A
19. A	**39.** All of the above
20. C	**40.** None of the above

Acknowledgments

First, my thanks to the actors, assistants, caretakers, and others in Hollywood who very generously gave me their anonymous takes on the industry. I am indebted to Edward Jay Epstein for producing his amazing book *The Big Picture: The New Logic of Money and Power in Hollywood* (Random House, 2005), which steered me down paths I otherwise wouldn't have considered. I was also greatly helped by three other books: *Open Wide: How Hollywood Box Office Became a National Obsession* by Dade Hayes and Jonathan Bing (Hyperion, 2004), *Hollywood, Interrupted: Insanity Chic in Babylon—The Case Against Celebrity* by Andrew Breitbart and Mark Ebner (Wiley, 2004), and *You'll Never Nanny in This Town Again: The True Adventures of a Hollywood Nanny* by Suzanne Hansen (Crown, 2005) The extraordinary website www.thesmokinggun.com was an invaluable tool for exploring interests and needs of celebrities through their court documents.

About the Author

STEPHEN P. WILLIAMS has written for the *New York Times, Men's Journal, Newsweek, GQ, Smithsonian, Martha Stewart Living,* and *Teen People.* He lives in New York City and is the author of *How to Be President.*